RENOIR

RENOIR

ANTHEA CALLEN

ORESKO BOOKS LTD·LONDON

(*frontispiece*)
Renoir Painting at Cagnes
Photograph: Roger-Viollet

ACKNOWLEDGEMENTS
My foremost thanks must go to the Leverhulme Trust, who financed my two years of post-graduate research in Paris and thereby provided me with the foundations for all my subsequent writings on French painting. I have a special debt to my thesis supervisor, Dr. R.W. Ratcliffe of the Courtauld Institute, whose enthusiasm inspired me to tackle the field of technique in the first place and who has given me vital clues and ideas, as well as friendly support. To M. Marc Havel, Ingénieur Conseil to Lefranc Bourgeois in France, I owe not only a wealth of knowledge about nineteenth-century painting methods, but also kindness and affection. Many other friends and associates have helped me in the writing of this book, in particular: Professor Julian Gardner of Warwick University provided me with valuable information concerning the Pompeian frescoes in Naples; Griselda Pollock read parts of the book in its early stages and gave me helpful criticism and encouragement; the Conservation Department of the Fitzwilliam Museum, Cambridge kindly answered my queries concerning their *Return from the Fields*. My thanks go to my editor Robert Oresko whose excellent work has produced the finished object, and to Elizabeth Marr who patiently extracted the illustrations from such far-flung collections.

Sincere thanks are also due to the following for their help in providing photographs and information: Art Gallery and Museum, Aberdeen; Art Institute of Chicago, Chicago; Barnes Foundation, Merion; British Museum, London; Chrysler Museum, Norfolk, Virginia; Cleveland Museum of Art, Cleveland; Courtauld Institute Galleries, London; Durand-Ruel collection, Paris; Fitzwilliam Museum, Cambridge; Fogg Art Museum, Cambridge, Massachusetts; Folkwang Museum, Essen; Glasgow Art Museum and Gallery, Glasgow; Joan and Lester Avnet, Palm Beach; Kunsthalle, Hamburg; Lefevre Gallery, London; Metropolitan Museum of Art, New York; Musée Fabre, Montpellier; Musée du Louvre, Paris; Musée du Petit Palais, Paris; Museu de Arte, São Paulo; Museum of Fine Arts, Boston; Museum of Fine Arts, Houston; Museum of Modern Western Art, Tokyo; National Gallery, London; National Gallery of Art, Washington; Nationalmuseum, Stockholm; National Museum of Wales, Cardiff; Norton Simon Foundation, Los Angeles; Oskar Reinhart 'am Römerholz' Collection, Winterthur; Philadelphia Museum of Art, Philadelphia; Phillips Collection, Washington; Portland Museum of Art, Portland, Oregon; Pushkin Museum, Moscow; Rijksmuseum Kröller-Müller, Otterlo; Staatliche Gemäldegalerie, Berlin; Staatsgalerie, Stuttgart; Städelsches Kunstinstitut, Frankfurt; M. Stavros S. Niarchos, Paris; Sterling and Francine Clark Art Institute, Williamstown; Toledo Museum of Art, Toledo, Ohio; Utrillo Collection, Vésinet; Wadsworth Atheneum, Hartford; Wallraf-Richartz Museum, Cologne; Ets. J. E. Bulloz, Paris; Photographie Giraudon, Paris; M. Claude O'Sughrue, Montpellier; Roger-Viollet Agency, Paris; and the Service de Documentation Photographique de la Réunion des Musées Nationaux, Paris. Finally, I would like to thank those collectors who have kindly given permission to reproduce works in their collections, but who have wished to remain anonymous.

Unless specified differently, all the works reproduced in this book are oil on canvas.

For my parents, Henry and Gertrude Young.

First published in Great Britain by
Oresko Books Ltd., 30 Notting Hill Gate, London W11

UK ISBN 0 905368 20 7 (cloth)
UK ISBN 0 905368 21 5 (paper)
Copyright © Oresko Books Ltd. 1978

First printed in Great Britain by
Burgess & Son (Abingdon) Ltd., Abingdon, Oxfordshire

Library of Congress Cataloging in Publication Data
Callen, Anthea.
  Renoir.
  (Oresko art book series)
  Bibliography: p.
  1. Renoir, Auguste, 1841–1919. 2. Painters—
France—Biography. I. Title. II. Series.
ND553.R45C32 1977 759.4 (B) 77–10354
US ISBN 0–8467–0377–7
US ISBN 0–8467–0378–5 pbk.

Pierre-Auguste Renoir

Early Formation

'. . . it is only since the Revolution that the principles of the old masters have been swept away . . . The old masters were taught each step of their trade, from the making of a brush and the grinding of a colour. They stayed with their teachers until they had learned well the ancient traditions of the craft. And the tradition has never been an obstacle to originality. Raphael was a pupil of Perugino; but that did not prevent his becoming the divine Raphael.' (Renoir quoted by Pach)

The French Revolution of 1789 was in fact only the final break following nearly 150 years' increasing erosion of the traditional craft training of the artist. Renoir here showed himself to be a traditionalist, and particularly, an artist sufficiently conscious of his place within that craft tradition of painting to bemoan its loss. Logically, Renoir also resented the changing patterns imposed by the new industrial society, and the often disastrous effects that mass-production and trade expansion exerted upon the materials of his craft.

Pierre-Auguste Renoir's respect for tradition was early manifested in his desire for a formal training at the Ecole des Beaux-Arts and his ambition for official recognition within the rigid career structure then open to French artists. He was the only one of his immediate friends to go to the Ecole, where records indicate that he attended classes and took examinations from the time of his admission to the painting section on 1 April 1862, until records of him cease just over two years later. Renoir's academic training was typical of the period for, in addition to his evening classes in drawing at the Ecole, he had sought out a painting teacher in whose atelier he could work regularly from the model and whose name would be influential in artistic circles. It now seems certain that Renoir enrolled at the Atelier Gleyre as early as October 1861, for in that month he registered, naming Gleyre as his teacher, at the Cabinet des Estampes, where artists copied from Renaissance drawings. Contrary to current popular opinion, Charles Gleyre was not an Academician, nor was he a professor at the Ecole; despite a traditional training and a note-worthy success at the Salon of 1843 which established his reputation, Gleyre was an independent and intro-spective character who led a life isolated from the ambitions of his academic colleagues. Similarly, his actual attitude to landscape differed greatly from common assumptions made about it today; far from being opposed to landscape painting, he considered it a 'highly eminent genre, and practised it throughout his career' (Boime). Gleyre in his youth had been friendly with Bonington, often working in the open air with him, in watercolours. Unlike most of his contemporaries, Gleyre did not discourage potential landscapists, but rather encouraged each of his students according to his individual bent. During the period when Renoir was his student, Gleyre was working on *plein air* 'studies in which he was absorbed by the play of natural lighting on the female figure' (Boime), a theme to which Renoir soon turned. These concerns undoubtedly influenced Renoir's choice of teacher, as it did that of his friends Monet, Sisley and Bazille, who all joined him at the atelier during the autumn of 1862.

An additional incentive to the young artists was the fact that Gleyre was one of the few teachers not to charge for his services but, remembering his own tough youth, merely asked his students for ten francs a month towards rent and the model. This must have been of particular value to Renoir, whose lower-middle-class artisan background was not one which was readily able to foster a talent such as his. He was born in Limoges, Haute-Vienne on 25 February 1841 into the large family of Léonard Renoir, a tailor by trade, and his wife Marguerite Merlet, a seamstress. In 1844 they moved to Paris where they settled in the heart of the old city, near the Louvre.

During his youth Renoir's aptitude for drawing was noticed, and from 1854 to 1858 he was apprenticed to a firm of porcelain painters, Lévy Brothers, rue des Fossés-du-Temple, where his talent did not go unused. When he decided to give up his work to become a professional artist, he was obliged to devote himself first to earning sufficient money to support himself and pay his Ecole tuition.

Among the porcelain services painted by Renoir was one based on Boucher's *Bath of Diana* of 1742 (Paris, Musée du Louvre), thus betraying his early preference for French eighteenth-century art and indicating that he was already familiar with copying from the Old Masters before he began his career as an artist. Renoir was therefore well prepared for this more personal aspect of a student's artistic training, and he was further encouraged to work in the Louvre by Fantin-Latour, whom he met in 1863.

fig. I Jean-Honoré FRAGONARD
The Bathers
Paris, Musée du Louvre

As David Wakefield points out in his *Fragonard*
(1976), this painting was in the La Caze collection and was given to the Louvre in 1869. It was
thus a painting with which Renoir would have
been familiar, and while stylistically and emotionally closer to the luscious nudes of his late
style, it must nevertheless have been in his mind
when he conceived *The Large Bathers* (Plate 72).
While in Renoir's painting the composition was
reversed, with the chief figures and foliage
weighted to the left and the water to the right,
the overall conception of sensuous nudity within
a lush landscape has strong links with Fragonard.

According to Frédéric Bazille, Gleyre visited his
students twice a week to criticize and advise them on
their progress, coming to each student in turn and
occasionally setting them a composition piece, either
drawn or sketched in oils depending on the individual's
stage of development; a student had to be perfectly
competent at drawing before being allowed to work in
oils. Gleyre considered painting to be a 'strictly manual'
side of the artist's trade, and his attitude may have
kindled Renoir's life-long feeling for craftsmanship; as
he stressed later: 'It was under Gleyre that I learnt my
trade as a painter' (Vollard). His family's skills must
also have engendered a healthy respect for craftsmanship.

With regard to painting Gleyre emphasized 'the need
for complete mastery of the brush to permit a spontaneous execution on canvas. Unhampered by the
manual requirements, the artist would be free to
concentrate on his modelling. Gleyre thus instructed his
pupils to prepare their palettes carefully, placing all the
necessary tones in order before touching the canvas'
(Boime). While the concept of spontaneous execution
was to have a lasting importance for Renoir, the
academic approach to pre-mixing the tones and laying
out the palette, which was the method of Renoir's idol,
Delacroix, ceased to have relevance as Renoir's colour
became more radical. Even at that time his interest in
colour, 'that devilish colour' which according to Gleyre

risked turning the student's head and as a result
sacrificing his drawn modelling, made Renoir appear
revolutionary. His sheer hedonistic pleasure in painting,
which was to become the central characteristic of his
art, was also startling to Gleyre, who, looking at his
work remarked coolly to the young artist: 'It's doubtless
to amuse yourself that you're doing a bit of painting?'
Renoir's reply came from the heart: 'Why, certainly,
and if it didn't amuse me, I beg you to believe I
wouldn't do it!' (quoted by André). In spite of what
seem like quite natural disagreements between the two
generations of artists, Renoir showed great respect for
Gleyre, far more than for Emile Signol, his staunchly
academic teacher at the Ecole. Thus, in virtually every
Salon up to 1870 in which Renoir exhibited, and
occasionally afterwards, he listed himself 'pupil of
Gleyre', even long after lack of funds and the master's
failing eyesight had caused the atelier to be closed, in the
spring of 1864.

The spring of 1863 was significant for Renoir;
following the standard training procedure and the
advice of Gleyre he headed out of Paris to the Forest of
Fontainebleau to begin making studies from nature, in
the company of Monet, Sisley and Bazille. Monet was
already comparatively experienced at painting *en plein
air,* having learnt much from working with Boudin and
Jongkind. But for Renoir, new to this method, Monet's
example was invaluable, as was the impact of new
friends among the older generation of landscape
painters.

The completely novel aspect of *plein air* painting
taught by Boudin to Monet, and passed on by him to
his friends, was that of finishing oil studies in front of the
subject or motif. Most of the older landscapists made
studies in oil from nature, but then returned to the
studio to complete them or reproduce them on a larger
and more 'finished' scale. Others, like Jongkind,
worked first in watercolour only, transferring the sketch
into oils in the studio. To the academic, the sketch was
synonymous with the unfinished and was therefore
primarily something to be used in preparation for a
finished painting, and so could not be seen as a complete work in its own right.

Thus the approach to landscape painting that Renoir
was learning on his first trip to Fontainebleau was
radical for the period, insisting as it did on the validity
and indeed superiority of the artist's spontaneous
perception of nature and the importance of capturing
this sensation on canvas with all speed and accuracy.
Although, unlike Monet, Renoir never devoted himself
entirely to landscape painting, nevertheless the character of his art during the 1870s was dominated by this
approach.

One artist of the older generation who took a liking
to Renoir, and who was to allow him the use of his
colour merchant's account, was Diaz, himself originally
a porcelain painter. Looking over Renoir's shoulder as

he worked in the forest Diaz apparently said: 'It's not badly drawn, but why the devil do you paint so black?' (Vollard). Hardly any of Renoir's paintings from this early period have survived, so it is difficult to assess the accuracy of this recollection. However, it is likely that, with a knowledge of older Barbizon paintings as his main model for landscape, his palette was at first dominated by a sombre tonal range, modulated by the use of bitumen and black. But by 1865, from which date works by Renoir do survive, the influence of both Corot and Courbet is discernible in his evolving landscape style.

Despite Renoir's interest in making landscape studies from nature, his major concern was with the figure, and was to remain so. Frequently, though, this concern coincided with his landscape work, in his recurrent preoccupation with solving the problems of painting the figure in an outdoor setting. Of his earliest surviving works, the largest number deal with the figure and many are portraits. Two portraits of 1864 stand out: first that of *William Sisley*, Alfred Sisley's father (Paris, Musée du Louvre) and second that of *Romaine Lacaux* (Plate 1). Particularly important in these two paintings is the superb use of focus, the sharp clarity of brushwork, which the artist exploited to direct the spectator's attention, in these cases to the head of the sitter.

In *Romaine Lacaux* the palette is muted, with an eye to the pearly greys of Corot and to the close-valued tones of Whistler's *White Girl* (Washington, National Gallery of Art), which had caused such a sensation at the Salon des Refusés of 1863. The pictorial space is shallow, reinforced by the frontality of the sitter, whose strength of character and forthright gaze are belied by her soft-textured surroundings and by the stable triangular shape she forms. The brushwork is tight on the face and looser elsewhere, creating a central ellipse of focus reminiscent of the area of focus of which the human eye is capable, leaving peripheral data hazy. Although appearing firmly located, the exact position of the figure of Romaine Lacaux within the limited pictorial space is ill-defined; there are no visual clues to lead the eye from foreground to back, and while the sweeping drape blocks off the left side of the picture, flowers push forward in the space at the right. The awkward thrusting angle of the chair-back, perhaps an attempted concession to spatial recession, fails to counteract the planal compositional design. The fluid, open brushwork varies from the thickly impasted highlights on the blouse to dry, scumbled sections, such as the skirt in the foreground, daringly underpainted yet highly successful thanks to his sharp emphasis on the face. This shallow, relief-like pictorial space became a distinctive feature of Renoir's mature work.

Early in 1865 Renoir probably met Jules LeCoeur, an architect-turned-painter who was one of the artist's closest friends during the following decade. LeCoeur had recently bought a cottage at Marlotte in the Forest of Fontainebleau, and he invited Renoir and Sisley to stay and work with him. Monet at this time was at nearby Chailly, doing preparatory landscape studies for his projected *Déjeuner sur l'Herbe* (Paris, Musée du Louvre, fragments only), and, considering the number of his fellow artists who were then attempting studies of figures in a landscape, it is hardly surprising to find Renoir setting himself the same problem. Although dated 1866, his *Portrait of Jules LeCoeur in the Forest of Fontainebleau* (Plate I) is a continuation of his interests at Marlotte during the spring and early summer of 1865, when he began preparing for the portrait. A study which survives for the forest motif, *Clearing in the Forest* (1865), shows remarkably similar handling, and was probably painted from the motif. Both in technique and in the choice of a dense, closely-wooded motif these two paintings reflect the artist's reaction to Courbet, whom he also met in 1865:

I painted two or three canvases with a palette knife, following the procedure dear to Courbet, and after that I painted with brushes heavily loaded ('en plein pâte') [see Plate 2]. I was perhaps successful in some parts, but I didn't find it convenient for re-working. It meant removing the spoilt parts with a knife, and I couldn't change a figure's position, at will, after the first sitting, without scraping the canvas. (Renoir quoted by André)

The paint and knife handling in Renoir's *Portrait of Jules LeCoeur* is more delicate and varied than the large, vigorous slabs typical of Courbet's palette-knife painting. In fact, despite the great difference in technique, the resultant image of LeCoeur links more, in the crusted effect of dappled sunlight caught here and there across the foliage, with the work of Diaz.

As early as 1864 Renoir, probably at the suggestion of Monet, had begun painting flower still-lifes. This genre provided, throughout Renoir's career, an area where he felt free to experiment without being hampered by the more demanding connotations of the human figure. Thus in his *Spring Bouquet* of 1866 (Plate 3) we find the artist freeing himself from the Courbetesque palette-knifed surfaces of the previous landscape works, and experimenting with a loaded brush and more fluid, richer paint, allowing himself a greater variety of marks enlivening the textures. Renoir described the experimental function of flower studies in his work:

I just let my brain rest when I paint flowers. I don't experience the same tension as I do when confronted by the model. When I am painting flowers, I establish the tones, I study the values carefully, without worrying about losing the picture. I don't dare do this with a figure piece for fear of ruining it. The experience which I gain in these works, I eventually apply to my [figure] pictures. (quoted by André)

Thus freed from the sombre greens and browns of Courbet, Renoir in his *Bouquet* showed a renewed joy in bright colours and a generally higher tonal key. While during the 1860s his concern for official recognition at the Salon, for the resultant security of buyers' and dealers' interest and for a growing reputation channelled Renoir's efforts into larger, more traditional paintings, by the early 1870s this delight in colour dominated his work.

In the early weeks of 1866 Renoir began a large composition, *The Inn at Mother Anthony's, Marlotte* (Plate 2), a group portrait which reaffirmed his interest in the human figure, and, moreover, elevated it to the monumental scale of Courbet. This large figure painting is an excellent example of the young artist's mastery of his *métier* by this date; the strong figures, placed in a solid triangular composition, reflect a knowledge of Manet's stark juxtaposition of blacks and subtle whites in the treatment of the fabrics. The eloquent handling of the superb still-life, similarly Manetesque, provides an excellent pause for the eye as it travels left around the group of faces and down the serving woman's arm.

During this period of extreme financial hardship Renoir was frequently forced to rely on the generosity of his friends for basic needs and painting materials. His brother Edmond recalled that Renoir even attempted to economize by grinding his own colours, but since such basic knowledge was lost to artists by this time, he soon abandoned the scheme.

It was probably in late 1865 or early 1866 that Renoir met Lise Tréhot through Jules LeCoeur, whose mistress Clémence was Lise's older sister. Lise, who was born in March 1848, was still in her teens when she began her relationship with Renoir; yet her full, unclassical rather Courbet-like figure, seen in *Diana*, was of the type to become so familiar in Renoir's painting.

Diana (Plate 7) was Renoir's first major Salon painting, and thus was an attempt to produce what he felt would be acceptable to the jury. He may have thought that with traditional subject matter and careful figure drawing, his realist tendencies might pass unnoticed, but although making a conscious effort to be conventional he was unable to hide his interest in Manet and Courbet. While the solid figure-type is closely linked to Courbet, the fluid painting and lack of half-tones in the modelling have more of the stark subtlety of Manet's *Olympia* of 1863 (Paris, Musée du Louvre), exhibited at the Salon of 1865. Renoir here returned to the use of the palette-knife, particularly in the landscape. The meticulous characterization of the silver birches on the right and of what looks like broom to the left of the figure placed Renoir amongst those who were preoccupied with the observation of nature rather than with its idealization. Yet the sense of artificiality in this studio picture is exaggerated by the contrasts between such detailed naturalistic observation and the 'stage-set' composition, and between the carefully controlled brushwork of the figure and the vigorous but often formless palette-knife work elsewhere, as in the rocks and the foreground. The figure, in a much higher tonal key than her surroundings, is perched in a precarious spatial relationship with rocks and ground,

her loincloth mooring her to the rocks while her left foot, just tucked behind the deer's fore-leg, acts as a planal anchor in the foreground. Thus again the relationship between figure and background is ill-defined and the pictorial space is shallow; one is reminded here of the typical Victorian photographic portrait studio where the painted backcloth provided a scenic but obviously two-dimensional backdrop. Renoir's *Diana* was refused by the Salon jury of 1867.

Visual evidence of Renoir's economic reliance on his friends is found in the extent to which he used them as models. In addition to his paintings of Lise, Renoir's portraits of Bazille and of M. and Mme. Sisley (Plate 10) date from this period. Of particular interest is his portrait of Bazille (Plate 5) in the studio they were sharing in the winter of 1867 on the rue de la Paix in the Batignolles quarter of Paris. This portrait, again close to Manet, shows the tall Bazille seated before his easel working on a still-life of dead birds and contains a wealth of technical information. Bazille is shown working here on a ready-made, ready-primed canvas, clearly indicated by Renoir's detailed brushwork on the exposed edge of the primed canvas where it is tacked onto the stretcher, and where the white of the ground is accentuated by Renoir's highlight. Ready-stretched canvases were available commercially from the 1840s in a large number of sizes, each strictly adhering to traditional proportions for the purpose required.

Just above Bazille's curved back is visible the reverse side of a canvas, turned against the wall to protect the painted surface from dust and revealing the skeleton of the stretcher. This particular model is a typical nineteenth-century French stretcher, with its square corner-joint, simple cross-piece for support and the nineteenth-century invention, the keys. Keys were small, flat wedge-shaped pieces of wood which could be tapped into the dry joints, forcing them open and tightening the canvas. Two keys can be seen in this exposed corner-joint in Renoir's painting, one in each side of the joint, overlapping each other, to distribute tension. A third, single key is just visible coming into the side joint of the cross-piece, from below, at a point where only one key is necessary.

Bazille's studio easel, of which only the base can be seen, whereon the artist's feet are lolling, is a particularly solid and expensive kind (no doubt symptomatic of his wealthy family's goodwill towards his painting), which was usually known as the *chevalet mécanique* or 'English' easel. This large adjustable studio easel, mounted on castors, was primarily intended for the execution of *grandes machines*, the large history paintings which were then on the wane, but it also provided a solid and lasting piece of studio furniture that could be adapted to take almost any size of canvas, often at a variety of angles (fig. 2). The metal support at the back of the easel can also be recognized in the manufacturer's diagram.

Modèle déposé, à châssis mobile, dit **Chevalet Anglais**.

fig. 2
Chevalet mécanique from the artists'
materials catalogue of Bourgeois Aîné, Paris,
April 1906. This is a studio easel of the type
used by Bazille in Renoir's *Portrait of Bazille*
(Plate 5).

P. Bazille 67

fig. 3 Frédéric BAZILLE
Still-life with Heron
Montpellier, Musée Fabre

This painting should be compared with the
version by Renoir in his *Portrait of Bazille*
(Plate 5).

Bazille's wooden palette is small and traditional in size; some artists used oval palettes, but the one here is shaped as if to fit into the lid of a travelling paint box, which may also be the reason for its size. By the nineteenth century, when artists used their palettes for mixing as well as holding their colours, the size of the palette became correspondingly large. Bazille's brushes appear extremely fine by contrast to the larger, stiffer hogs-hair ones which were then popular for use with thick tube colours. However, a glance at the *Still-life with Heron* (fig. 3) that Bazille was painting while posing for this portrait indicates that he was working in a tighter, more detailed technique than Renoir's loose, delicious summary of it suggests; the study Renoir shows Bazille painting would have been impossible to execute with the brushes he depicts in his sitter's hands. Clipped onto the palette, near Bazille's protruding thumb, are two small metal containers or *godets* which usually held oil (linseed or poppy, etc.) and turpentine spirit, to facilitate the adjustment of paint fluidity during execution.

When the brilliant greens of spring were still fresh on the trees along the Seine in Paris in 1867, Renoir followed the lead of Monet, trying his hand at *plein air* cityscapes. While Monet tackled dramatic and bird's-eye views, Renoir typically concentrated on calmer viewpoints, concerned as ever to explore his relationship with older masters in this tradition, from Canaletto to Corot. His panoramic study of *The Pont des Arts* (Plate 8), a 'modern life' record of crowds of pleasure-seekers bustling on the quai, was jotted down with a lively speed and Boudinesque accuracy and with brilliant touches of pure colour, emerald green, vermillion, enlivening an otherwise bright but fairly conventional palette. There are surprises, however, for in the long stretch of shadow in the foreground, cast by the Pont du Caroussel in the shade of which the artist was working, Renoir observed that the warm afternoon sun, yellowish, is producing not a neutral, but a cool mauvish-blue shadow, the coloured sunlight's opposing and therefore complementary hue on the chromatic circle. Observation of changing light and its effect upon colour in nature became a crucial element in Renoir's mature work.

The fact that this concern was already present is confirmed by another painting of that same year. *Lise with a Parasol* (Plate 12), which was painted in Chantilly in the summer of 1867 and shown at the Salon the following year, elicited this astute review from the critic Thoré-Bürger:

The dress of white gauze, enriched at the waist by a black ribbon whose ends reach to the ground, is in full light, but with a slight greenish cast from the reflections of the foliage. The head and neck are held in a delicate half-shadow under the shade of the parasol.

The effect is so natural and so true that one might very well find it false, because one is accustomed to nature represented in conventional colours ... Does not colour depend upon the environment that surrounds it? (quoted by Rewald, 1973)

It is as if, at least until 1873, there were two contradictory but parallel threads running side by side in Renoir's work; on the one hand he was experimenting with avant-garde *plein air* techniques, and on the other he was continuing a dialogue with tradition and the masters of the past. Around 1869–70 Renoir made a copy of Rubens's portrait of *Hélène Fourment and her Children* (Paris, Musée du Louvre), while as late as 1875, commissioned by the Delacroix-lover Jean Dollfus, he copied Delacroix's *Jewish Wedding in Morocco* (Paris, Musée du Louvre). The latter is particularly significant in view of Renoir's admiration for Delacroix and of his own treatment of North African themes, subjects which were, incidentally, extremely popular at the Salon and may have been used by Renoir for this very reason. Thus, even his *Bohemian* or *Lise* (Plate 11) of 1868, although an outdoor subject, can be seen as remarkably close to certain popular academic paintings, such as Henri Regnault's *Salomé* (fig. 4), which was a star attraction at the Salon of 1870.

More firmly rooted in the genre are Renoir's two large harem interiors of 1870 and 1872. *Odalisque* (Plate 16) which was shown at the Salon of 1870 along with *The Bather* (Plate 15) was openly in admiration of Delacroix, with its juxtaposition of warm orange-reds and blues and the rich variations in fabric texture from heavy metallic embroidery to light transparent gauze. The later painting, *The Harem (Parisian Women Dressed as Algerians)* (Plate 17), one of the last for which Lise posed, is cloying in its attempted narrative and fails as an unpleasant compromise between a creative interpretation of Delacroix and a sop to appease the Salon jury, by whom it was rejected in 1872; it appeared in the Refusés of that year.

Parallel to this more traditional approach, Renoir was coming again under the influence of Monet's *plein air* technique. During the summer of 1869 they worked together in the countryside near Paris, Renoir staying first with Lise at his parents' house in Ville d'Avray and later with Monet at nearby Bougival. The artists achieved together a series of sensational *plein air* studies of the bathing place at La Grenouillère, on the Seine near Bougival, which was to provide the foundations of the Impressionist method.

fig. 4 Henri REGNAULT
Salomé
New York, Metropolitan Museum of Art
(gift of George F. Baker)

Salomé was shown at the Salon of 1870 and can be compared with Renoir's *The Bohemian* (Plate 11), *The Harem* (Plate 17) and *Odalisque* (Plate 16). Renoir's paintings come close to the popular, though much slicker, academicism of Regnault.

Renoir and Impressionism

If I painted in light colours ('clair'), it is because one had to paint in light colours. It wasn't the result of a theory, but of a need, a need which was in the air, with everyone, unconsciously, not only with me. In painting in light colours I wasn't being revolutionary ... And the official artists with their bitumen were mad. One must be mad to want to stop the march of time. (Renoir quoted by Jean Renoir)

'... we don't eat every day. Yet I am happy in spite of it, because, as far as painting is concerned, Monet is good company. I do almost nothing because I haven't much paint' (Poulain). Such was Renoir's plight in the autumn of 1869, and it shows the typical good spirits he retained throughout. For almost every painting done by Renoir during his stay at La Grenouillère, there is a similar view by Monet (fig. 5). Four canvases by Renoir are known from this campaign, three illustrated here (Plates 18, 19 and II) and a fourth in a Milwaukee private collection (Rewald 1973, p. 231). These paintings show a dramatic contrast to his early sombre forest views (Plate I) and his *Pont des Arts* (Plate 8); there is a much greater sense of direct confrontation with the subject, rather than, as in the earlier work, a cool distant perspective. The brushwork is freer and broader, while avoiding the backdrop quality of his outdoor figure paintings.

The treatment of detail is cursory, necessitated in part by the demands of a rapid painting technique for recording the moment, but it gives a far more vibrant impression of the casual stir of an actual event. In the Moscow version (Plate 18) the figures in the foreground beside the river provide the main centre of interest, but are not artificially emphasized by Renoir's earlier device of sharpening the focus on key areas; instead the brushwork is more uniform and for almost the first time in Renoir's work he allowed the painting to breathe and speak directly to the spectator, rather than manipulating him. There is also a stronger feel for observed play of natural light, aided here by the example of Monet, in the rendering of dappled sunlight on the bank and the clothes and in the more awkward attempts to summarize the sensation of light reflecting off moving water. The stiff, slightly dry, dragged quality of the top layer of paint, for example in the figure, far left, would suggest that the colours were used straight from the tube, without thinning with turpentine or smoothing with oil, both of which take time.

The distribution of oil paint in collapsible tin tubes was an important though not crucial factor in the development of *plein air* painting. The collapsible tube was invented and patented in London in 1840, and although it was rapidly put into production in England, the continental manufacturers were slower to react. As late as 1855 the largest manufacturer in France was still charging extra for oil paints sold in collapsible tubes

fig. 5 Claude MONET
La Grenouillère
New York, Metropolitan Museum of Art
(H.O. Havemeyer collection)

Renoir's views of the same subject (Plates 18,
19 and II) were painted side by side with
that of Monet in the summer of 1869. More
experienced in the rendering of natural light
at this date, Monet showed a greater fluency
and strength of handling and a more plastic
description of space than Renoir.

rather than bladders. Where the average price for a
bladder of oil colour was about twenty-five centimes,
the extra five for a tube was a luxury. Lack of tin tubes
had done nothing to daunt earlier enthusiasts of the
plein air oil sketch, but obviously the superior practi-
cality of the tube did make prolonged outdoor work
more viable. Renoir later rather exaggerated the case:

Colours in tubes, being easy to carry, allowed us to work completely from nature. Without paint in tubes there would have
been no Cézanne, no Monet, no Sisley or Pissarro, nothing of
what the journalists were later to call Impressionism. (quoted by
Jean Renoir)

But it is extremely unlikely that Renoir ever used a
bladder, so he would not have had personal experience
of its problems.

Certain features already present in the paintings of

La Grenouillère are characteristic of the mature
Impressionist style. The overall tonality grew increasingly light, with conventional dark shadows
dispersed by the penetrating brightness observed in the
natural effects of sunlight. The palette itself became
more intensely colourful, using a restricted range of
basic colours. At this date Renoir still used tube black,
but by the first half of the 1870s this was no longer
compatible with his Impressionist palette, based on the
traditional tube colours nearest to the three theoretical
primaries and greens. Renoir spoke out much later
against the misuse of black: 'Shadows are not black; no
shadow is black. It always has colour. Nature knows
only colours . . . White and black are not colours'
(quoted by Rewald, 1973). White was the pigment used
by the Impressionists as a metaphor for light, often
predominating in colour mixtures, extending their
brilliance and opacity and therefore their capacity for
reflecting light from the picture surface into the eye.
This reflective power of colour with white gives the
paintings an increased luminosity. During the 1880s,
however, Renoir gradually moved away from opaque
colours to transparent ones which, in conjunction with
white grounds, produced a jewel-like depth and
brilliance.

Finish, or rather lack of finish, was another technical aspect central to the new depiction of nature. In order to capture the fleeting moment within the rapid flux of natural light effects, speed of execution and deftness in painterly calligraphy, abbreviating the observed world in legible visual shorthand, were essential. Lack of finish, as we have seen, was associated in academic circles with the preparatory sketch and with spontaneity; as such, both were perfectly acceptable, but neither was considered adequate without the ordering influence of the intellect. This artificial division inherent in nineteenth-century French art and thought, between mind and matter, theoretical and perceptual, extended into the realms of the practical, where the split between the intellectual activity of painting and practical craftsmanship was all but total. Renoir's concern with the materials of his craft was rare, but his anti-intellectual, anti-theoretical stance meant that he confirmed rather than contradicted the split. For the Impressionists, perceptual sensation of nature, the individual, spontaneous response, and its translation into paint with a sketchy lack of finish were all central concerns.

The most characteristic method of paint application in Impressionist painting, the small, broken, individual touch of colour, is, in purely technical terms, the best way to place colour down rapidly, especially when a single sitting is planned, and retain its pristine intensity of hue; any excessive working of the wet colours would quickly produce a muddy mess. Visually, the broken brushstroke simulates the flickering effect of light and movement in nature, particularly when used in conjunction with the white or pastel grounds so loved by these artists. Once past his early, sombre period, Renoir abandoned the common nineteenth-century dark ground, usually a warm brown or red, for the luminosity of white. Manet had been the first of the new generation to use white grounds, while Courbet still adhered to the old method. Among the landscapists, Boudin, Daubigny and Jongkind all preferred white grounds, though occasionally, when working on panel, chose to allow the warm wood colour to play through their brushwork, as had Corot. The majority of Renoir's mature works were executed on a white ground, though he often used pastel shades in the 1870s.

During the early 1870s Renoir worked frequently with his friends: in 1871, after the Franco-Prussian War and the Paris Commune, with Sisley at Bougival and in 1872 with Monet at Argenteuil. But Renoir remained essentially a Parisian, with his studio in the rue Notre Dame des Champs, and a visitor to the countryside. In Paris he had much less difficulty in finding models and getting the occasional portrait commission, and while Monet, Sisley and Pissarro concentrated almost exclusively on *plein air* landscape painting, Renoir was always more committed to the human figure, particu-larly the female one. The 1870s were for Renoir a period when pure colour transformed his palette, and he made numerous efforts to combine his love of the solidity of the figure with the often contradictory demands of a *plein air* study. Renoir rarely painted winter scenes; apart from the famous *Skating in the Bois de Boulogne* of 1868 (Basel, estate of Robert von Hirsch) and two or three other studies of snow made on the spot about the same period, he avoided working in the cold, which he hated. Moreover, the emotional warmth and optimism basic to his art were more accurately displayed in the glowing radiance of hot sunlight and the vibrant colours of summer.

Direct work from the motif is seen in action in Renoir's depiction of *Monet Painting in his Garden at Argenteuil* (Plate 38), in which Monet is shown painting in typical *plein air* style. Here the special portable tripod easel, the *chevalet de campagne*, which when not in use folded or collapsed to a nominal size, replaces its weighty studio counterpart (Plate 5). This rather flimsy structure was often made with sharply pointed feet to enable the artist to push it securely into the ground, and the canvas was usually weighted down to prevent its sudden disappearance in a gust of wind. The weather here must have been comparatively calm. Monet's canvas, exposed towards us along the left edge, reveals ready white-primed canvas as it continues round the side of the stretcher; although the size of the brushes is unclear, Monet does hold several alongside his paint-box-shaped wooden palette. His paint box, smallish for travelling, lies casually open on the ground beneath the easel, its multicoloured contents abbreviated in Renoir's representation. Beside it an elongated whitish patch can be identified as Monet's white painting umbrella, for use in sunlight to eliminate reflections from the wet paint surface; the partially overcast sky shown by Renoir must have caused insufficient reflections to warrant Monet using it.

Cheap, thin canvas and inadequate paints were the inevitable result of lack of funds, and it was only towards the mid-1870s that Renoir began to establish a small circle of admirers who would occasionally buy a painting or commission a portrait. It was sometime in March 1872 that Renoir met Paul Durand-Ruel, the Parisian art dealer who became famous for his early allegiance to this group of struggling painters. In fact it seems strange that the dealer did not meet Renoir sooner, for Monet and Pissarro had met him two years previously in London, where Durand-Ruel exhibited their works at his gallery in New Bond Street in the winter of 1870. However, Renoir's *Pont des Arts* (Plate 8) was acquired by Durand-Ruel in 1872 for 300 francs, and shown at the London exhibition in the winter of that year. This indicates that of all the group, Renoir was until that time receiving the least support; but during that year, thanks probably to the sales he made to Durand-Ruel, he was able to move into a large studio at 35 rue Saint-Georges.

The mood behind Renoir's decision to help organize unofficial group shows was desperation rather than rebelliousness. The official exhibition structure around the annual Salon was by the early 1870s too old-fashioned and rigid to accommodate change, and the evolution of a new structure of patronage, based principally on dealers and private collectors, was already under way. Thus the historic first group show of 1874, during which the critics dubbed the exhibitors the 'Impressionists', appears less startling when seen within a broader context. State and aristocratic domination of the art market was being superseded by a larger middle-class clientèle with freshly-filled purses and new tastes. For the artist, fame depended on the impact of a single, sensational painting at the Salon each year, the product of months of careful preparation and one among thousands. This, for the lucky few, would then lead to critical acclaim and rich amateurs.

While the Impressionist group shows were similarly concerned to establish the artist's reputation, they based their efforts on smaller, less individually pampered paintings rather than the often unsaleable Salon ones. The artists tended to produce their paintings more rapidly and so needed to sell more, initially at lower prices, and they hoped, by showing their work whenever possible, to build up a discerning group of amateurs, willing to pay increasingly good prices. The size and subject matter of their works were especially suitable for middle-class apartments, but most amateurs were scornful and afraid to buy something novel until it had received the approval of the Salon jury.

Unlike most of his friends who exhibited regularly with the group, Renoir retained his conviction in the necessity of official recognition as the best means to fame and fortune. He submitted work to the Salon jury assiduously, only failing to send in 1876 and 1877; he also continued to send paintings to the Impressionist group shows, and his dual exhibition policy frequently caused friction with his colleagues who felt his attitude expressed disloyalty. Renoir was, however, determined to succeed no matter what the cost. He wrote to Durand-Ruel in the spring of 1881, from Algeria, trying to explain his reasons for exhibiting at the Salon:

There are in Paris hardly 15 amateurs capable of appreciating a painter outside the Salon. There are 80,000 who wouldn't even buy a nose if a painter is not at the Salon. That is why I send two portraits every year, however little that may seem. (quoted by Venturi, vol. I)

But far from compromising his art for the sake of acceptance, Renoir emphasized that his work was improving, and he assured Durand-Ruel:

I want to make you wonderful paintings that you will sell very expensively . . . Have patience, and in a short while I hope to give you proof that one can both submit to the Salon and do good painting.

The following year, 1882, when Durand-Ruel attempted to re-unite the splintered group for the seventh Impressionist show, Renoir followed Monet's lead in refusing to participate. Renoir told his dealer that if he chose to exhibit paintings he owned, there was nothing the artist could do to stop him. But at a moment when Renoir saw himself at last gaining public approval, he considered that exhibiting with newcomers and radicals like Gauguin would reduce the value of his canvases by half. Renoir's most ardent early amateur was Victor Chocquet, a passionate admirer of Delacroix, and, via Renoir, of Cézanne. Renoir met Chocquet after the Impressionist sale of 1875, and he commissioned several portraits of himself and his wife (Plates 40 and 39), feeling that Renoir's painting and love of colour had strong similarities with those of his beloved Delacroix.

By the mid-1870s Renoir had eliminated black from his palette, except for its occasional use in such works as the *Portrait of Mme. Charpentier and her Children* (Plate 48) of 1878. The dark shadows and foliage in his landscapes, such as *The Gust of Wind* (Plate 29) of 1873–74 and *Fisher with Rod and Line* (Plate 30) of c.1874, were achieved by the use of dark transparent greens, produced with viridian often in direct mixture with similarly transparent blues such as French ultramarine. He would often intensify the depth of this coloured shadow or dark by adding a rose madder (alizarin), and this is clearly visible in *The Gust of Wind* where the colours were rapidly laid in and only partially mixed. The Impressionists were quick to recognize that dark hues could be created by the combination of more or less complementary colours, and that even the partial mixture of a red and a green pigment would produce a far more colourful dark than would the 'dead' quality of a black used direct from the tube to darken a hue. *The Gust of Wind* is interesting in that it was painted on a pale beige-coloured ground. Canvases primed in a variety of shades could then be bought ready-prepared commercially; pastel colours of brown, grey, pink, yellow and blue were commonly available, and the very fact that manufacturers began mass-producing coloured grounds implies both a wide-spread usage, and acceptance of a sketch-like *facture,* through which such grounds could reverberate. In *The Gust of Wind* the warmth of the light beige ground is accentuated by the juxtaposition of cool, slightly acid greens playing loosely over it on the open hill area; thus the ground functions here to evoke the sense of sunny warmth and the dryness of the summer hillside in contrasting warm and cool hues.

The use of a white or pastel ground was one of the key factors in the heightened luminosity of Impressionist paintings. Loose brushwork increased the visual interplay between paint and ground, enabling the artist to create more convincingly the sensation of the passing moment and capture the changing quality of light in nature with a new spontaneity. *Fisher with Rod and Line*

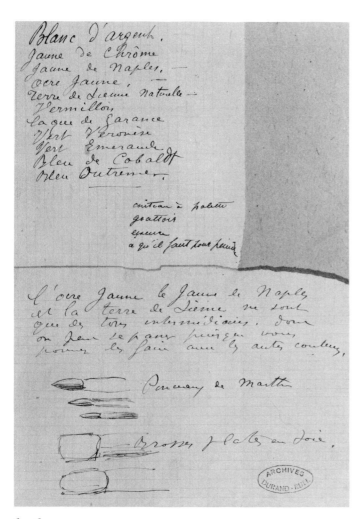

fig. 6
List hand-written by Renoir of his
Impressionist palette and materials, probably
dating from c. 1877, from the Durand-Ruel
Archives, Paris.

from the tube; touches of rose madder appear with the viridian to give extra depth to the shadow at the base of the bush, close to Renoir's signature. The highlights of water reflection are worked in amongst the wet viridian, in thick white impasto. This painting is a particularly stunning example of the technical virtuosity and sheer inventiveness of Renoir's Impressionist period. The bright tonal key and the overall vigour of the brushwork bring the image close to the picture surface, emphasizing its plasticity and creating a flowing subtle rhythm as the eye moves in and out across the surface. Already by this date Renoir was preoccupied with the potential of transparent oil colours, seeking to exploit the richness of luminosity produced by delicate washes and pure transparent paints over opaque grounds. This method reached its purest development in Renoir's late work. The evident need for speed of execution in the *plein air* Impressionist technique resulted in the adoption of a ground which was particularly absorbent and upon which a first lay-in with turpentine-diluted paint would dry very rapidly, permitting work to progress without delay.

Renoir's materials during his Impressionist period were recorded by him in a document, now in the Durand-Ruel Archives, Paris (fig. 6), which probably dates from the second half of the 1870s. In translation it reads:

Flake White	Rose Madder [alizarin]
Chrome Yellow	Emerald Green
Naples Yellow	Viridian Green
Yellow Ochre	Cobalt Blue
Raw Sienna	French Ultramarine
Vermilion	
palette knife	
scraper	
turpentine	
what you need for painting	

Yellow Ochre, Naples Yellow and Raw Sienna are only intermediary hues thus one can do without them because they can be made with other colours. Fine marten-hair brushes, flat hogs-hair brushes.

Renoir's son Jean recalled that he had never seen his father using chrome yellow, and it is evident from what Renoir himself said that he did not use it for long:

I formerly used chrome which is a superb colour, but which can, it appears, play nasty tricks. I tried cadmium yellow; I found great difficulty in using it; it made me paint heavily. Then, I wanted to do my little Rubens. I began to paint with Naples yellow which is a rather dull colour. It gave me all the brilliance that I was looking for. But it's always the same story . . . it depends on what I put around it. (quoted by André)

Although it had great covering power and brilliance, chrome yellow was a bad mixer and also tended to go brown with age. Renoir's colour merchant and paint grinder, M. Moisse at Mulard's, rue Clauzel, and, after 1904, in his own shop in the rue Pigalle, confirmed that Renoir had never asked him for cadmium yellow, thus suggesting that the artist's experiments with this colour took place before about 1878, when Renoir

(Plate 30) is a rapidly executed painting, done from the motif, probably in a single sitting. The ground is again beige, providing a warm colour bias which accentuates the cool greens of the foliage. Detail is kept to the minimum, with vivid colour accents, like the pure vermilion decoration on the woman's hat, serving to punctuate a limited range of ochres and greens. An initial, thin lay-in of paint, through which the ground is still visible, establishes the basic hues of grass and foliage; then the technique varies. The footpath leading into the painting on the left was made simply by rubbing the damp lay-in with a rag to expose more of the light ground; this seems to have been a fairly late adjustment, intended to echo the river and give a greater sense of space to the left side of the composition. A similar rag-rubbed method was used to give form to the torso of the male figure, then touches of muted, white-dominated vermilion and black were added. In places the dragged paint caught only on the ridges of canvas, while in others the rubbing left the colour only deep in the crevices. The staccato dabs of paint in the foreground, describing the dark foliage hanging over the water, again use unmixed viridian, stiff and dense

15

began buying his colours from Mulard. According to Moisse, Renoir also experimented briefly with zinc yellow around 1899. It is significant that Mulard's speciality was the hand-grinding of colours, which were then sold in tubes, and Jean Renoir recalled having seen half-a-dozen or so young women in white blouses grinding the colours by hand in the workshop; by this date most manufacturers had installed modern machinery for grinding pigments, but Renoir refused to use anything but the traditional materials. Before 1878 it seems likely that Renoir bought his colours from Père Tanguy, whose shop was next to Mulard's in the rue Clauzel. Renoir certainly knew him by 1875, when he took Chocquet to this shop to see the paintings by Cézanne that Tanguy had there, given in exchange for materials; but it is possible that Renoir had known Tanguy from the mid-1860s when the colourman had peddled his wares around the artists' haunts of Fontainebleau. It seems unlikely, however, that Tanguy's reputedly thick ground coarse pigments would have appealed to Renoir, whose love of fluid oil paints was already evident by the mid-1860s, although a paint grinder as generous as Tanguy must have been a boon to a struggling, impoverished artist such as Renoir was up until the second half of the 1870s.

Renoir used this palette during the 1870s to study and translate the effects of sunlight on the figure, as well as for landscapes. In particular he seemed to be fascinated by the distorting and dissolving effects of dappled sunlight as it flickered through leaves onto figures beneath. In these paintings Renoir explored the abstracting qualities of sunlight, which produce arbitrary patterns of light and shade cutting across solid form and eroding it, emphasizing decorative surface design to the detriment of conventional modelling in the figure. Renoir was to reject this preoccupation in the 1880s, recalling critically: 'While painting directly from nature, the artist reaches the point where he looks only for the effects of light, where he no longer composes, and he quickly descends into monotony' (quoted by Rewald, 1973). In fact it is obvious even from his work of the 1870s that Renoir was composing all the time, more or less intuitively, but compared to the increased self-consciousness of his work of the 1880s his earlier pictures seemed to him formless.

In *Woman's Torso in Sunlight* (Plate IV) the natural environment of the figure is sketched in freely and in places seems, due to the effects of flickering sunlight, to overlap the nude. The artist gives no clues as to what happens below her drape; no spatial provision has been made for her legs, either standing or sitting. The figure is cramped and crowded in a limited claustrophobic setting. She was described by the unsympathetic critic Albert Wolff, when the painting was shown at the second Impressionist exhibition of 1876, as a 'mass of flesh in the process of decomposition with green and violet spots . . .' (quoted by Rewald, 1973). The figure

is delicately transformed by the coloured patches of sunlight and shade, which create a rhythmic surface pattern and break up the roundness of the form. But, unlike Monet, Renoir never treated his figures as if they were of no more importance than the landscape; on the contrary, here the figure is the central element which, although seen in terms of sunlight, is nevertheless rendered in tighter, more careful brushwork than the foliage.

The Swing of 1876 (Plate 42) shows Renoir again tackling the problem of figures in natural sunlight, and here the treatment becomes more decorative and less dependent on observation; that is, he adjusted things to suit his overall conception. During 1876 Renoir rented a second studio at 12 rue Cortot in Montmartre, and it was in its gardens that he painted *The Swing*, using his friends for models, and in the nearby grounds of The Moulin de la Galette that he painted his large canvas *Dancing at The Moulin de la Galette* (Plate 43) that same year. In *The Swing* Renoir used short brushstrokes to describe the broken pools of sunlight and to create an arbitrary rhythm of warm and cool contrasting colours across the canvas. The decorative aspect is accentuated by the rhythmic loops of dotted light weaving up the path on the right side of the painting and by the unnaturalistic omission of shadow cast beneath the male figure in the foreground. Similarly, the even reflection of sunlight from the white dress of the model on the swing, Jeanne, was thus depicted for compositional emphasis, while the reflections from the white-smocked child to the left were toned down to avoid distracting the eye.

Dancing at The Moulin de la Galette explores the same contrasts of sunlight and shade, warm and cool colour as *The Swing*. The canvas was painted from the motif; Renoir's friends helped him to carry it out and set it up each day. The sunlight is again indicated by soft patches of alternate warm and cool colours, floating across clothes, faces and the ground amongst the figures. The changing scale of figures lends a sense of space, but the splashes of colour and emphatic brushwork bring the composition up close to the picture surface, creating a scintillating network of colour and represented light. Three years later in Renoir's *The End of the Lunch* (Plate 45) there is comparatively little feel of the outdoor setting. Although obviously not posed in direct sunlight, the light on the figures is even and flat, while the backdrop treatment of the foliage combines with it to give an interior feel to the group; the bland, shadowless quality of the light may, however, have been the product of a bright but overcast sky.

Renoir's *Luncheon of the Boating Party* (Plate 53) situated at the restaurant Fournaise, Chatou, is the last of his great *plein air* Impressionist group studies. The figure of Aline Charigot to the left with her dog remains delicately Impressionist, but the study of Caillebotte in the right foreground already exhibits a new, more restrained touch. *The Umbrellas* (Plate 63) of

1881–86 is more obviously an amalgam of old and new styles, begun as it was at the earlier date, and reworked, the main female figure to the left in particular, after Renoir's stylistic transformation.

By the end of the 1870s Renoir began to reconsider the direction of his work, feeling a dissatisfaction that was to cause a revolution in his style and technique, a dissatisfaction that was felt by all his Impressionist friends and which created a general stylistic crisis during the 1880s. In Renoir's Impressionist figure paintings, colour and modelled form seemed mutually exclusive, and his figures are Impressionist at the expense of his love of solid form; he refused to make this concession in the 1880s, and then in his late work resolved the split and achieved a fusion of the two elements.

Travel and Change

I so much like a thing that Cézanne said once: 'It took me forty years to find out that painting is not sculpture.' That means that at first he thought he must force his effects of modelling with black and white and load his canvases with paint, in order to equal, if he could, the effects of sculpture. Later, his study brought him to see that the work of the painter is so to use colour that, even when it is laid on very thinly, it gives the full result. (Renoir quoted by Pach)

Renoir might almost have been talking here about his own dilemma between traditional chiaroscuro modelling and the colouristic build-up of form he was to achieve by his late years. His relationship with Cézanne in the 1880s was important to the development of the art of both men. By this time Renoir was turning away from what he saw as the insubstantiality of Impressionism, concerned as it was with capturing fleeting effects of light and atmosphere, and for him Cézanne was the only artist among his contemporaries who could offer the example of a search for something consciously structured and timeless in painting. Cézanne, while exploring Impressionist luminosity and pure colour, had been recognized by his fellows as having a more classical approach to painting:

M. Cézanne is, in his work, a Greek from the *belle époque*: his canvases have the calm, the heroic serenity of antique paintings and terra-cottas . . . the movements of the figures are simple and grand like antique sculpture, the landscapes have an imposing majesty, and his still lifes so beautiful, so precise in their relationship of colour values ['tons'], have a solemnity in their truth. (Georges Rivière, 1877, quoted by Venturi, vol. II)

Renoir was familiar with Cézanne's work from the group shows and from the collection of their mutual patron Chocquet, and he owned several works himself. In May 1880 Chocquet commissioned Renoir to do a pastel *Portrait of Cézanne* (New York, Ittleson collection) which Cézanne subsequently copied, and this seems to have promoted the close relationship the two artists were to enjoy during the 1880s.

In addition to a shared admiration for Delacroix and Rubens and a general respect for the Old Masters, they also liked each other's painting, and Cézanne's copy of his pastel portrait by Renoir probably indicated a desire to learn from the latter's advanced colour technique. The two artists worked together regularly during the 1880s; Cézanne is said to have criticized Renoir's paintings for being 'cottony' and to have encouraged him to develop a more tightly organized picture surface. Several of Renoir's landscapes and figure studies of this period, such as *The Return from the Fields* (Plate 67), show direct quotations from Cézanne's directional, block-like brushstrokes, though often transformed by Renoir's use of thin veils of colour (fig. 7). This method can be seen in many of Renoir's paintings from his Italian trip, such as the superb still-life of onions painted in Naples (Plate 55), and for several years afterwards the structured, hatched brushwork gave new strength to his rhythmic, colourful paint surfaces.

Renoir's trip to Italy in the winter of 1881–82 was similarly important in the transformation of his style in the early 1880s. Already in the spring of 1881 he had begun his travels with a brief visit to Algeria with his friend Frédéric Cordey, from which his *Field of Banana Trees* dates (Plate 52). It is evident that at this period Renoir was happy to leave the problems of Paris behind him. So it was with his Italian voyage; Renoir was bored with working continually on society portraits and the need to flatter his sitters. After the success of *Mme. Charpentier and her Children*, which was well-placed at the Salon of 1879 thanks to Mme. Charpentier's powerful influence, Renoir had been in increasing demand as a portraitist, but it was not an area in which he felt free to push forward and experiment, and he often felt uncomfortable among upper-class clients with a superior attitude to his 'common' manners. He also believed that a traditional-style pilgrimage to Rome and the works of Raphael would give him new prestige and distinction from his Impressionist friends and silence the critics who unjustly called him a revolutionary; he wrote from Venice: 'Now I will be able to reply bluntly yes, Monsieur I have seen the Raphaels' (quoted by Florisoone).

Although Renoir was at first rather cynical about going to see the Raphael frescoes in Rome, he was impressed by them; he wrote to Durand-Ruel from Naples in November 1881: 'They are indeed beautiful and I should have come to see them sooner . . . I prefer Ingres in oil painting. But the frescoes are admirable in simplicity and grandeur' (quoted by Venturi, vol. I). In the same letter Renoir discussed the progress of his own work, which was the major reason for his trip: 'I am still suffering with experiments. I am not satisfied, and I scrape off and scrape off again . . . But I think I will have made progress, which always comes after long experiments. One always returns to one's first loves, but with something extra.' Thus, far from abandoning

fig. 7 Paul CÉZANNE
View of the Château de Médan
Glasgow, Glasgow Art Gallery and Museum,
Burrell Collection

This picture was probably painted in 1880
when Cézanne stayed at Zola's country house
in Médan. The so-called 'constructive stroke'
of Cézanne is clearly visible here, but the
structured, parallel strokes used a rich impasto
by contrast to Renoir's thin washes, which
may indicate that Renoir was more influenced
by Cézanne's watercolours of this period.

his preoccupation with light and colour, Renoir was
searching for a way to reconcile his Impressionist
luminosity with his old love of solid female form and to
combine the two into a new, monumental whole.

The first large-scale figure composition in which this
new monumentality appears is Renoir's *Blond Bather*
(Plate 58), which may have been posed by Aline
Charigot, and which is thought to have been completed
in Naples in 1881. Here the form is no longer dissolved
by the effects of dappled sunlight, but is, by contrast,
posed under a high, blanching, unifying Mediterranean
sun. Contour plays a key rôle in giving a taut strength

of edge to the form, as conventional tonal modelling is
virtually non-existent. In the limited areas of shading
on the body a delicate colour-contrasting grey-blue-
green serves to depict cast shadow. Sea, rocks and hair
are constructed from touches of opposing warm and
cool colours, increasing the vibrant harmony of the
surface and emphasizing the smoother bulk of the
figure.

Despite Renoir's knowledge of mural techniques and
his concern to see the Raphael and Pompeian frescoes,
they seem to have influenced the evolution of his new
style only marginally. The simplified grandeur of their
figures was a vital inspiration to him in his search for a
new figural monumentality, but so no doubt were
Cézanne's figures too. It seems crucial that what
Renoir chose to see in Raphael was light: 'Although
Raphael never worked outside he did study sunlight as
his frescoes are full of it' (quoted by Florisoone). He
stressed that he too was studying the sunlight of the
south which, unlike the cool northern light of Paris, was
constant and thus enabled him to 'efface and begin over
again as often as I wish. That is the great teacher, and in

fig. 8 Jean-Auguste-Dominique INGRES
The Source
Paris, Musée du Louvre

Renoir admired Ingres all his life, mentioning
in particular the gentle swell of the belly in
this painting. While he respected the grandeur
of the Raphael frescoes in Rome in 1881, he
stressed that he preferred Ingres in oil
painting. The influence of this master can be
seen in Renoir's figure painting of the 1880s,
such as *The Large Bathers* (Plate 72).

Paris I am obliged to be content with so little.' Through
this study in constant sunlight Renoir claimed he was
learning to re-create the grandeur of the ancients; in
Raphael he was able to find a justification for his own
concern with light. The monumentality that Renoir
loved in the frescoes was for him a result of the same
process of simplification he observed the figure under-
going in the harsh, nearer vertical sunlight of the
Mediterranean and which he captured in his *Blond
Bather*. Cézanne believed in the value of looking,
particularly under southern light, and he may have
prompted Renoir to follow suit; it does seem clear from
the evidence that Renoir felt he had more to learn from
studying nature under steady sunlight passing through
its daily arc than he had from the frescoes themselves.

While it seems apparent that on a broad conceptual
level Renoir wanted his major work of the 1880s,
The Large Bathers (Plate 72), to be seen within the
tradition of monumental wall decoration—its full title
originally included 'essay in decorative painting'—it is
unlikely that Renoir was at this period attempting to
imitate a fresco technique in oils. There is no record of
his admiring the actual techniques he saw in Italy, and
he even stressed his preference for Ingres's work in oils.
Barbara White discusses one painting, *Portrait of Mme.
Renoir* (Philadelphia, Philadelphia Museum of Art,
c. 1885), where the 'underpainting appears to be a thin
white plaster coat, presumably gesso'; Renoir, who was
familiar with Cennino Cennini's early fourteenth-
century treatise on painting *Il libro dell' arte*, would
have known that gesso was a ground used in early
Italian panel painting and not in fresco, where the
pigments were mixed with water and painted onto a
wet plaster of sand and lime and were literally cemented
into position by the chemical conversion of the lime into
calcium carbonate. Furthermore, when Renoir saw
them in 1881–82, the Pompeian frescoes in the Museo
Nazionale, Naples would not have shown any technical
similarity to Renoir's paintings; first, these frescoes
were smoothed flat by the Pompeians with hot irons
while still wet, producing a surface unbroken by brush
texture, in contrast to the rich, tactile surface of
Renoir's oils. Secondly, the frescoes were at that time
covered by a thick protective layer of wax, which would
have dulled the surface, making the colours dark and
subdued.

Renoir's unconventional 'gesso' ground mentioned
above was not made in imitation of fresco technique but
rather to provide a smooth, opaque surface capable of
maximum light reflection; Renoir explained later that
he preferred coarse canvas, thinking it more durable
than fine, but to obliterate the canvas texture would
have required such a thick layer of ground. It is
likely that this ground was in fact of the type described
by Jean Renoir, oil-based rather than gesso and used in
varying degrees of thickness depending on the effect the
artist sought. This ground was made from flake white
mixed with one-third linseed oil and two-thirds
turpentine spirit and after its application had to be left
for several days to dry; often Renoir would ask for the
amount of oil to be increased which, though it took
longer to dry, produced an even smoother ['lisse'] paint
surface. This ground can be seen quite clearly in

fig. 9 Suzanne VALADON
Self-portrait
Vésinet, Utrillo Collection

The contrast between this analytical self-portrait and Renoir's idealizing of his model can be seen in *The Large Bathers* (Plate 72), for which Suzanne Valadon posed, probably the two figures on the left and in the centre.

fig. 10 François GIRARDON
Nymphs Bathing
Versailles

This low-relief sculpture from the ornamental pond in the Allée des Marmousets in the park at Versailles provided Renoir with both compositional and structural inspiration for his *Large Bathers* (Plate 72).

Renoir's *The Return from the Fields* (Plate 67), where he worked on a ready-made canvas size 15 (54 × 65 cm.), which careful examination shows to have been ready-primed. On top of this white ground a second, smooth layer of priming covers the canvas grain over most of the canvas and was applied with a knife. Although a chemical analysis has not been made to confirm the composition of this ground, visually it appears too 'greasy' a surface to be anything but oil-based. Gesso is a very fine, matt, absorbent ground, water-based and glue-bound, which would have quickly sucked up the juicy washes of oil colour used by Renoir. However, in *The Return from the Fields* the wash-like paint slides across the smooth white surface achieving a high degree of transparency even among the earth colours, as the ground reflects the light back through them, a method significantly close to that of overglaze porcelain painting.

Typical of Renoir's new style of painting was the return to the composed, studio picture. Already in his letters of 1882 there are allusions to this, for when writing to Durand-Ruel about the delay in sending his dealer his Italian canvases, he emphasized that he had 'indispensible retouchings' to do in Paris. The following year Renoir wrote to him from Guernsey: 'I hope to return soon . . . with some canvases and documents to make some paintings in Paris . . . I hope, despite the few things I shall be able to bring back, to give you an idea of these charming landscapes' (quoted by Venturi, vol. I). Thus his larger, more highly finished paintings from this trip, such as *By the Seashore* (Plate 65), were doubtless painted in his studio after his return to Paris. The seascape in *By the Seashore* was probably based on direct study, perhaps one of the 'documents' he mentioned; but there was no longer a concerted effort to integrate figure and background. As in the *Blond Bather* there is a tighter, more Ingresque rendering of flesh, a feature which reaches its height in his so-called 'harsh' style of *The Large Bathers* (Plate 72) of 1887.

Renoir spent three years preparing his *Large Bathers*,

which caused a sensation among his fellow artists when it was first shown at Georges Petit's Gallery in 1887. Pissarro wrote to his son Lucien: 'I do understand what he is trying to do, it is not proper to want to stand still, but he chose to concentrate on line, his figures are all separate entities, detached from one another without regard for colour.' Berthe Morisot had written more enthusiastically the previous year of Renoir's progress in this new style:

Visit to Renoir's studio. On an easel, a drawing in sanguine and white chalk [e.g. *Nude Woman*, Plate 74] from a mother breast-feeding her child; charming grace and finesse. As I admired it, he showed me a series after the same model, more or less in the same spirit. He is a draughtsman of first-rate strength; all his pre-paratory studies for a painting would be curious to show to the public who generally imagine that the Impressionists work only in the most free and easy manner. I think that one cannot go further in the rendering of form, two drawings of naked women going into the sea charmed me to the same degree as those of Ingres. He [Renoir] tells me that the nude seems to him one of the indispensible forms of art. (quoted by Rouart)

Berthe Morisot, who was as conservative as Renoir, was more able to applaud his new tendencies than was the radical Pissarro.

The Large Bathers, in which Renoir tried consciously to bring himself closer to the opulent eroticism of eighteenth-century French painters, Fragonard and Boucher in particular, in fact took its composition from a low-relief sculpture by François Girardon (1628–1715), the *Nymphs Bathing* from the ornamental pond in the Allée des Marmousets at Versailles (fig. 10), which Renoir reversed and changed to his own requirements. It seems by no means accidental that Renoir should have been inspired by a low-relief in this painting, which was similarly conceived in terms of a shallow 'sculpted' modelling of the figures and in the limited, relief-like pictorial space within which they are frozen. The treatment of landscape relies much more on con-vention than on his usual observation of nature. It was at this period that Renoir, reversing his earlier position, again advocated the use of tube black, 'queen of colours' as he called it.

After the birth of his first child, Pierre, in 1885,

Renoir gradually began to settle to a more homely life-style, often feeling happy to concentrate on subjects suggested by his own family (Plate 76). By the late 1880s Renoir's style had become less arid as his painting went again into a period of transformation towards the relaxed and luxuriant 'iridescent' style of his late years.

The Late Years

He retained from his first *métier* of painting on porcelain the taste for light and transparent colours. The white ground of his canvas today plays the rôle which the kaolin of his plates once did. (André)

Albert André described the painting technique of Renoir's late period:

He attacks his canvas, when the subject is simple, by tracing with a fine soft brush, usually with an earth red, a few very summary indications to see the proportions of the elements which will constitute his painting.

This can be seen in the unfinished *Coiffure* (Plate 75) for which Gabrielle posed in c. 1895–96: here raw sienna rather than earth red was used to outline the round, full arms and the position of the hands, the 'volumes' as he would say. 'Then immediately, with pure colours diluted with turpentine as if he were using watercolour, he would scumble the canvas rapidly and one could see something imprecise, iridescent appear, the colours merging into one another, something which one found ravishing even before understanding the sense of the image.' At the second sitting, 'once the turpentine had evaporated a little, he would work over that prepara-tion, proceeding in virtually the same manner, but with a mixture of oil and turpentine and a little more pigment.'

In Renoir's *Garden at Cagnes* (Plate 77) and in the delicious *After the Bath* (Plate 87) this fluid oil wash technique is boldly visible. In both the strong texture of the canvas grain is clearly apparent, with the paint flowing into its crevices leaving the tips of the white ground vibrating through the colour. The use of multiple veils of transparent, jewel-like colour, de-scribed by André, can also be seen here, increasing in their degree of pigmentation and opacity in the more worked areas of these pictures. Along the bottom edge of *Garden at Cagnes* free washes of paint gathered in fluid waves, like a tide-mark. Renoir's shadows were now fully transparent, evoking the Rubens he loved, but using pure, saturated colour reminiscent of early Italian panel painting. In *After the Bath* Renoir attained a harmonious unity, particularly between figure and background, which had previously eluded him. And it was through this luminous wash technique, exploiting to the full the physical properties of his materials, that Renoir finally achieved this mastery without losing the solidity of the figure. At last he was able to free himself from stylistic preoccupations and allow the purely painterly to take over.

By this date, Renoir rarely mixed his colours on his palette, which was rectangular and fitted into the lid of his paint box and which was always kept immaculately clean. He would carefully squeeze economical blobs of tube colour around the outside edge of his palette, while in the two *godets* clipped on near his thumb-hole he used first pure linseed oil and secondly an equal mixture of that and turpentine. Beside him he would keep a jar of turpentine in which he rinsed his brush after practically every brushstroke, in order to retain maximum purity of colour. Unlike Monet, for example, Renoir used few brushes at a time throwing out any that were worn or dripped and might impede his precision of touch. To clean his palette, the artist would first scrape it and burn the waste; then he rubbed it with a rag soaked in turpentine until no trace of colour was left. His brushes were washed in cold water and soap, the bristles being rubbed gently in the palm of the hand.

Renoir's colour merchant, M. Moisse, commented on the similarity of Renoir's late palette to that of twenty-five years previously; looking at his records for 1895, he said:

Here is his order for January: Flake white, antimony [Naples] yellow, cobalt blue, viridian green, ivory black, raw earth [Sienna], yellow ochre, superfine carmine. That for February: Naples yellow, raw Italian earth, Venetian red. That for April: flake white, Naples yellow, yellow ochre, raw earth, carmine, cobalt blue, French vermilion. That for July: flake white, Naples yellow, viridian green, cobalt, rose madder [alizarin] . . . Now, that's exactly the same type of order as he made in the last years. (quoted by Tabarant)

Jean Renoir recalled that towards the end of his life Renoir simplified his palette even further, describing the order in which his father laid out his palette for *The Bathers* of 1918 (Plate IX) in his studio at Les Collettes:

Starting from the bottom, near to the thumb-hole: the flake white in a plentiful 'sausage', the Naples yellow in a little 'turd' like all the following colours: yellow ochre, raw Sienna, red ochre, rose madder, green earth, emerald green, cobalt blue, ivory black. This choice of colours was not immutable. I have on rare occasions seen Renoir use Chinese vermilion, which he placed between the rose madder and the green earth.

The reds were crucial to the iridescent palette of this period; Renoir said: 'I want a red to be sonorous, to sound like a bell; if it doesn't turn out that way, I put more reds or other colours till I get it . . . I look at a nude; there are myriads of tiny tints. I must find the ones that will make the flesh on my canvas live and quiver' (quoted by Pach). It was with the reds above all that Renoir painted for the future. He was very concerned about the durability of his paintings, wanting them to last well, and anticipated that they would need a good fifty years to 'break in'; he feared painting only for the present, as in his youth when certain paintings had blackened. He said: 'A painting must be able to withstand varnish, dirt and all the dishonesties to which time and restorers may subject it' (quoted by André). After 1900, Renoir was sufficiently wealthy to have his choice of materials, and he would frequently work on unstretched canvas which he bought in great rolls upwards of a metre in width and from which he cut lengths to suit each individual project.

The two paintings of dancers (see *Dancer with Castanets*, Plate 80) which were made for the apartment of Maurice Gangnat in the summer of 1909, were both painted on specially cut canvases, and in order for the crippled artist to reach the upper sections, his chair was installed on trestles. For his portraits, such as that of the dealer Ambroise Vollard (Plate 78), Renoir usually turned to ready-made canvases, in standard 'portrait' dimensions; Vollard's portrait was executed on a size 25 canvas. Occasionally he would also use standard, prepared canvases for his imaginative subjects, such as *The Judgement of Paris* (Plate 79), which is on a canvas size 40. Vollard reported Renoir as saying that his preoccupation with still-lifes of roses, from the mid-1890s, was his way of experimenting with flesh tints for his nudes, such as those in *The Judgement*.

From 1900 onwards, Renoir was increasingly paralysed by rheumatism and eventually had to have his brush strapped to his wrist; he enjoyed shocking the curious, who refused to believe how he continued painting, with the emotionally not inaccurate maxim: 'it's not with his hand that he paints, but with his . . . [penis]!' Despite tremendous difficulties, the quality of his work was even more rich and sensuous than before. Jean Renoir's description of his father's methods is symptomatic of the artist's triumph over his disability:

. . . a painting began with incomprehensible touches on the white ground, not even forms. At times the liquid, linseed oil and turpentine spirit, was so abundant compared to the pigment that it would run on the canvas. Renoir called that the 'juice' ['le jus']. Thanks to this juice he could, with a few brushstrokes, establish a first general tonality. That covered more or less the whole canvas, or rather the whole surface of the future painting, as Renoir often left parts of the white ground untouched. These marks constituted for him the indispensible colour values. It was essential that the ground was very pure and very smooth . . . Little by little, strokes of rose or blues, then raw Sienna, would intermingle with perfect harmony. Usually the Naples yellow and rose madder were introduced only later, the ivory black at the end. He never proceeded with angles or lines. His 'handwriting' was rounded as if following the contour of a young woman's belly.

No doubt Renoir's flowing colour and line were in part a function of the limitations placed upon him by his debilitating illness.

'For my part,' he said, 'I have always avoided being a revolutionary, I always believed and I still believe that I have only just continued what others have done and much better before me' (quoted by André). Unlike Monet, Renoir never sought to challenge accepted notions of painting and avoided the self-consciously intellectual or analytical in his work. He saw himself as part of a tradition of French painting, not as someone breaking free of it, a modernist: 'I think that of all my many paintings enough will remain to assure me a place in the French School, that school 1 love so much, which is so gentle, so light, such good company . . . And not rowdy' (quoted by André). Renoir's conservatism and his love of traditional subject matter, particularly the nude, have tended to obscure the more experimental characteristics of his art. Like his avant-garde companions, he was concerned with a shallow pictorial space and a flattened, decorative paint surface; his composition was much less daring than Monet's, but his conventional use of the figure did not permit a more abstracted compositional design. In his experimentation with colour, however, Renoir was among the most innovatory of his generation, first in exploring the potential of brilliant, pure colours, using contrasting cool and warm hues to model form, and secondly, slowly developing the most luminous, transparent palette of all his contemporaries but Cézanne.

To the last Renoir was above all a craftsman, committed to his *métier*, and constantly open to change:

I love paint to be oily, unctuous, as smooth as possible. It's for that reason that I love oil paintings so much. To arrive at the results I have been searching for . . . and that I seek still, I've tried every process . . . I could never be reproached for shutting myself up in a system. (quoted by André)

Bibliography

André, Albert, *Renoir*. Paris, 1919, 1923, 1928.

Bodelsen, M., 'Early Impressionist Sales 1874–1894', *The Burlington Magazine* (June 1968).

Boime, Albert, *The Academy and French Painting in the 19th Century*. London, 1971.

Carson Webster, J., 'The Technique of Impressionism: A Reappraisal', *College Art Journal* (1944–45).

Centenaire de l'impressionnisme (catalogue of the exhibition at the Grand Palais, Paris). Paris, 1974.

Champa, Kermit S., *Studies in Early Impressionism*. New Haven and London, 1973.

Cooper, Douglas, *The Courtauld Collection*. London, 1954.

Cooper, Douglas, 'Renoir, Lise and the LeCoeur Family', *The Burlington Magazine* (May; September–October 1959).

Daulte, F., *Bazille et son temps*. Geneva, 1952.

Daulte, F., *Renoir: Catalogue raisonné de l'oeuvre peint (Tome I: Les Figures (1860–1890)*, first of four volumes). Lausanne, 1971.

Davies, Martin, *National Gallery Catalogues: French School*. London, 1970.

Drucker, M., *Renoir*. Paris, 1944.

Florisoone, M., 'Renoir et la famille Charpentier', *L'Amour de l'Art* (February 1938).

Ingamells, John, *The Davies Collection of French Art*. Cardiff, 1967.

Laurie, A. P., *The Painter's Methods and Materials*. New York, 1967.

Lethève, J., *La vie quotidienne des artistes français au XIXe siècle*. Paris, 1968.

Meier-Graefe, J., *A. Renoir*. Paris, 1912.

Le livre d'art ou traité de la peinture par Cennino Cennini . . . (translated by Victor Mottez; introductory letter to Henry Mottez, by Renoir). Paris, 1911.

Pach, Walter, *Queer Thing, Painting*. New York, 1938.

Poulain, G., *Bazille et ses amis*. Paris, 1932.

Reff, Theodore, 'Copyists in the Louvre, 1850–70', *Art Bulletin* (December 1964).

Renoir, Jean, *Renoir*. Paris, 1962.

Rewald, John, 'Auguste Renoir and his Brother', *Gazette des Beaux-Arts* (March 1945).

Rewald, John, 'Chocquet and Cézanne', *Gazette des Beaux-Arts* (July-August 1969).

Rewald, John, *The History of Impressionism*. London, 1973.

Rey, Robert, *Renaissance du sentiment classique*. Paris, 1931.

Rivière, Georges, *Renoir et ses amis*. Paris, 1921.

Rouart, Denis, *Correspondance de Berthe Morisot*. Paris, 1950.

Rudorf, R., *Belle Epoque: Paris in the '90s*. London, 1972.

Shiff, Richard, *Impressionist Criticism, Impressionist Colour and Cézanne* (unpublished doctoral thesis for Yale University, 1973).

Sterling, C. and Salinger, M. M., *French Paintings: A Catalogue of the Metropolitan Museum of Art*. New York, 1967.

Tabarant, A., 'Couleurs', *Bulletin de la Vie Artistique* (1923).

Venturi, L., *Les archives de l'impressionnisme*, 2 volumes. Paris and New York, 1939.

Vollard A., *Auguste Renoir*. Paris, 1920.

White, Barbara E., 'Renoir's Trip to Italy', *Art Bulletin* (December 1969).

1 *Portrait of Romaine Lacaux*

CLEVELAND (OHIO), Cleveland Museum of Art (Hanna fund). 81 × 64 cm. Signed and dated centre right: A Renoir 1864.

This early portrait demonstrates Renoir's youthful powers and his sensitivity to fabric texture. The grain of the canvas can be seen cutting through the light brushwork of flowers near the upper right-hand edge.

(*above left*)
2 *The Inn at Mother Anthony's, Marlotte*
STOCKHOLM, Nationalmuseum. 193 × 130 cm. Signed and dated lower right: Renoir 1866.

The models for this painting were, from left to right: Nana, Jules LeCoeur, an unknown man, Mother Anthony, Sisley. On the wall is a caricature, painted by Renoir himself, of Henry Murger, author of the famous *Scènes de la vie de Bohème*. Even when they were not staying at the Inn, Renoir, Sisley and LeCoeur went there regularly to eat in the evenings; the dog, Toto, also appears in the *Portrait of Jules LeCoeur* (Plate I). Renoir recalled the setting of this painting: 'The subject of this picture is the common room, which doubled as a dining room and lounge . . . The "motifs" in the background of the picture were borrowed from sketches actually painted on the wall—these "frescoes" unpretentious but often quite successful were the work of the artist habitués of the place' (quoted by Vollard). Courbet's *After Dinner at Ornans* (Lille, Musée des Beaux-Arts, 1849), which treats the figures on a similar monumental scale, was probably the inspiration for Renoir's painting. The influence of Manet is also visible here, and while not a prescribed element of an artist's training in the 1860s, the study of his near-contemporaries was an unavoidable factor in a young artist's development. Study of the Old Masters was considered essential, but a thorough understanding of the most recent innovations was not formally recognized, particularly if it involved the work of radicals like Courbet and Manet. Yet it was crucial for the more adventurous to 'work through' avant-garde painterly statements to absorb their relevance before moving on to a more personal style. For Renoir, whose facility for change and adaptation of other styles made him more rather than less experimental, this involved an exhaustive exploration of the work of his elders, stylistically, technically and in terms of subject matter, which lasted until the late 1860s. Although begun during the winter of 1865, *The Inn at Mother Anthony's* was probably only completed after Renoir had begun sharing Bazille's new studio in the rue Visconti in July 1866. He may have hoped to have it ready for the Salon of that year.

(*above right*)
3 *Spring Bouquet*
CAMBRIDGE (MASSACHUSETTS), Fogg Art Museum (bequest of Grenville L. Winthrop). 106 × 80 cm. Signed and dated lower right: A Renoir 1866.

Using the same size canvas as for the *Portrait of Jules LeCoeur* (Plate I), Renoir here made an ambitious experiment in bright colours and a fluid, impastoed oil paint, in a genre that was to provide him with an endless source of technical ideas.

(*opposite*)
4 *Spring Bouquet*, detail of Plate 3

The varied and painterly brushwork which Renoir used here is reminiscent of that in similar studies by Delacroix and is a reminder of the importance of this colourist in Renoir's evolution.

5 *Portrait of Frédéric Bazille*
PARIS, Musée du Louvre. 105 × 73·5 cm. Signed and dated lower right: A Renoir 67.

This portrait was admired by Manet and entered his collection, either as a gift of Renoir or perhaps bought to aid the younger artist. The canvas texture is visible in the white area of Bazille's still-life, along the edge of his painted canvas; cracking can be seen on Bazille's chair, and the specificity of its location indicates a fault in that particular colour, perhaps caused by the faster drying of a layer of turpentine-mixed colour over slower-drying, oilier paint. The painting hanging on the wall behind Bazille has been identified as a snowscene by Monet, who was sharing Bazille's Paris studio at this date. Bazille died young in 1870, while in action during the Franco-Prussian war.

(*above left*)
6 *Portrait of Mme. Théodore Charpentier mère*
PARIS, Musée du Louvre. 1869. 46 × 38·4 cm. Signed centre right: A Renoir.

The subject of this portrait is Madame Marie-Pauline Charpentier (1802–1875), née Le Grand, mother of Marie Charpentier who was married to Charles LeCoeur, brother of Renoir's friend Jules. This unusual little painting, executed in slightly dry, crusty scumbled oils, is a superb study of an ageing woman. The canvas grain is clearly visible, especially in the light background.

(*above right*)
7 *Diana*
WASHINGTON, National Gallery of Art (Chester Dale collection). 196 × 131 cm. Signed and dated lower right: A Renoir 1867.

Renoir's mistress Lise Tréhot posed for this major early figure piece, which was rejected by the jury at the Salon of 1867. Renoir here used traditional subject matter, which was typical of his approach to painting in the 1860s when, while hoping to gain acceptance through the use of academic themes, his technique and conception by contrast placed him firmly among the realist avant-garde. While in the *Portrait of Jules LeCoeur* (Plate I) the genre used is that of the hunting scene, *Diana* has an even more academically oriented pedigree; but Renoir produced a straight-forward, unclassical nude study which was transformed by the addition of symbolic items, a bow, a dead deer pierced by an arrow, a sheaf of arrows, in a landscape setting, into the goddess of hunting.

8 *The Pont des Arts*

LOS ANGELES, Norton Simon Foundation. 1867. 62 × 103 cm. Signed lower right: A Renoir.

One of the first of his studies of modern life, Renoir here focused the main visual activity into the lower centre portion of the canvas, on a line with the gently descending silhouettes of the Palais Richelieu and the Institut de France, home of the Académie, with the Pont des Arts forming a dark line at an erratic eye-level. This canvas format, which is particularly long and narrow, is unusual in Renoir's *oeuvre;* the dimensions conform closely to those ready-prepared canvases then offered by colour merchants called *marine haut* or 'upright marine'. Renoir evidently chose this especially elongated format—only *marine base* or 'horizontal marine' provided a narrower one—to suit the low view-point, panoramic vista he planned to paint.

(*opposite*)

9 *The Pont des Arts,* detail of Plate 8

It is evident that many of the figures in the middle ground were added later, after the initial layer of paint had dried, as brushstrokes from this earlier layer, which represents the sun-drenched quai, remain unslurred beneath the paint of the figures. This can be seen here in the striding male figure with the cane and the woman and child to the right. It was common practice, even during the Impressionist years, to add in later small colour accents and details of interest to pull together a composition and provide a sense of scale. The final work on the sky was also late, as the paint along the horizon was worked in around the finished buildings. Slight cracking can be seen in the heavy impasto of the sky here, emphasizing the likelihood of over-working in this area.

10 *Portrait of M. and Mme. Alfred Sisley*
COLOGNE, Wallraf-Richartz Museum. 1868. 105 × 75 cm. Signed lower left: Renoir.

The confidently painted figures have a rather uneasy relationship with their outdoor setting; the figure of Sisley in particular seems to have troubled Renoir, causing him to exploit the stripe on his right trouser leg to separate Sisley from the background, which softly encroaches on the couple. There is heavy *pentimenti* or scarring in the upper third of this painting, perhaps indicating the re-use of an old canvas.

11 *The Bohemian* or *Summer* (*Lise*)
BERLIN, Staatliche Gemäldegalerie. 1868. 90 × 62·5 cm. Signed lower left: Renoir.

This theme may have been suggested by Murger's *Scènes de la vie de Bohème*, which was well-known and with which Renoir must have been familiar because of his caricature of the author (Plate 2). However, Renoir had his eye on Salon success, and this type of subject was very popular with the public. In this painting and in several others of the period, including the *Portrait of M. and Mme. Sisley* (Plate 10), Renoir was exploring the visual properties of striped fabrics. One obvious quality is the emphasis that stripes give to solidity of form and the way they accentuate changing planes in the pictorial space. Although Renoir later 'homogenized' his female types rather more, at this date Lise, facially at least, is perfectly recognizable in Renoir's many studies of her. This painting should be compared with the photograph of Lise reproduced in Cooper, 1959. However, Renoir frequently took liberties with the colour of her hair.

(*above left*)

12 *Lise with a Parasol*

ESSEN, Folkwang Museum. 182 × 118 cm. Signed and dated lower right: A Renoir 67.

While being Renoir's first major *plein air* figure study, *Lise* nevertheless has a traditional pedigree which links it to English eighteenth-century portraiture. Here, however, the landscape simply provides a setting, by contrast to the earlier English prototype which normally incorporated a careful portrait of the wealthy sitter's estate, and it is treated with a cursory lack of definition in soft, fuzzy brushwork. The sunlight reflected from Lise's white dress illumines her neck and chin and, where the dress is shaded by her parasol from the strong, warm light, contrasting touches of cool bluish paint transform the white of the fabric. Because it was painted in the open air, *Lise* shows greater naturalism and a much softer, gentler touch than Renoir's *Diana* (Plate 7). *Lise* appeared at the Salon of 1868.

(*above right*)

13 *The Clown*

OTTERLO, Rijksmuseum Kröller-Müller. 194 × 136·5 cm. Signed and dated lower right: A Renoir 68.

Desperately in need of money, Renoir accepted this commission in the winter of 1867–68. 'Renoir painted a picture for the Café du Cirque d'Hiver. The prearranged price was 100 francs. The owner of the show went bankrupt and the picture remained in the artist's possession' (Meier-Graefe). This extraordinary, Manetesque painting, although spatially unsatisfactory, is nevertheless an ambitious attempt to produce in oils something sufficiently powerful to act as an advertisement. There seems to be here a second, partially obscured, signature, and possibly an inscription; the artist may have erased some dedication pertinent to the commission after it fell through.

14 *Nymph at the Source*

LONDON, National Gallery. c. 1869. 66·5 × 124 cm. Signed lower right: A Renoir.

Although there has been much dispute over the dating of this work (cf. Davies), it is not possible to date it to the 1880s. The facial features are close to those of Lise in *The Bohemian* (Plate 11), but the figure is much slimmer than as she appears in *Diana* (Plate 7), which could perhaps be ascribed to a lessening of the influence of Courbet in the later study. Firmer evidence for the pre-Impressionist dating is the traditional palette used here by Renoir, with its affinities to that of *Diana* and *Lise with a Parasol* (Plate 12). Finally, the signature is of a type common to the 1860s and early '70s; the initial 'A' he only rarely used later, the jerky, stubby 'R' soon gave way to a rounder one, while the flamboyant 'r' at the end of the signature was also shortlived. His mature signature became more compact and sensuously curved. The face here has strong technical similarities with the more finished head of Mme. Darras (Plate 22), dated 1871, and in these two the hands are more alike than those in *Diana*; but there is an awkward naivety in the *Nymph* which suggests it predates Renoir's work at La Grenouillère with Monet and leads me to place it in the early summer of 1869.

16 *Odalisque*
WASHINGTON, National Gallery of Art (Chester Dale collection). 68·5 × 123 cm. Signed and dated lower left: A Renoir 70.

Both *The Bather* (Plate 15) and the *Odalisque* were posed by Renoir's young mistress, Lise.

(*opposite*)
15 *The Bather with Griffon*
SÃO PAULO, Museu de Arte. 184·2 × 114·9 cm. Signed and dated lower right: A Renoir 70.

Exhibited at the Salon of 1870 along with the *Odalisque* (Plate 16), *The Bather* still owed something to Courbet, perhaps even the motif of the moored boat and riverside setting which evoke the older artist's *Young Women beside the Seine* (Paris, Petit Palais, 1856). In Renoir's painting less is left to the imagination, as while one girl looks on, the other takes off her clothes ready to bathe; the scene is less shocking than Manet's *Picnic on the Grass* (Paris, Musée du Louvre, 1863), where the nude's clothed companions are male. Compared to his earlier *Diana* (Plate 7), *The Bather* has a soft, gentle touch more reminiscent of Corot, particularly in the treatment of the foliage. Renoir completely abandoned his earlier palette knife technique, and the rather harsh tonal contrasts and rendering of the figure in *Diana* were replaced by a more characteristic, visible, directional brushstroke which echoes the form and models it. His brushwork in the *Nymph* (Plate 14) is similar but looser; a tighter technique as in *The Bather* was essential to Salon success.

17 *The Harem (Parisian Women Dressed as Algerians)*
TOKYO, Museum of Modern Western Art. 155 × 130 cm. Signed and dated lower left: A Renoir.
1872.

This is one of the last paintings posed by Lise before her marriage on 24 April 1872 to the young
architect Georges Brière de l'Isle, after which she is thought never to have seen Renoir again.
Here the artist again chose an oriental subject in the hope of gaining Salon acceptance. The
picture is based upon a dynamic diagonal composition, with an explicit narrative element
linking the foreground figures to the girl in the background. Technique, subject and detail, with
their sumptuous evocation of rich texture, are reminders of Renoir's debt to Delacroix, while the
crass sentimentality shows closer links with contemporary treatment of such themes, like Henri
Regnault's *Salomé* (fig. 4). This is Renoir at his most 'camp'.

18 *La Grenouillère*
MOSCOW, Pushkin Museum. 1869. 66 × 79 cm. Signed lower left: Renoir.

La Grenouillère, literally The Frog Pond, was a highly popular Second Empire bathing place and boating centre, served by a restaurant which is visible to the far right of the Stockholm version (Plate II). It was situated on the small arm of the Seine at Croissy, near Chatou, where Renoir painted *Luncheon of the Boating Party* (Plate 53) at the restaurant Fournaise, and not far from Bougival further upstream, in the other direction. 'Near Chatou the two branches of the river are crossed by the Paris-Saint-Germain railroad, France's first, which stops at Rueil, on the right bank of the Seine' (Rewald, 1973). Thus spots like La Grenouillère were of easy access to the Parisians seeking fun and leisure. The crowds under the trees and in the water and all the varied effects of sunlight around them provided excellent motifs for *plein air* study. This painting is particularly interesting as proof of the artist's poverty; a close look indicates that this work was painted over a previous, quite heavily impasted painting, which is visible where the direction of the underneath work cuts through a new area, for example the criss-cross of marks across the two main figures, centre left, and the similar lines in the bottom right-hand corner. The figure at the far left is also hastily and only partly covering earlier dry paint. The mature signature here is a later addition.

19 *La Grenouillère*
WINTERTHUR, Collection Oskar Reinhart 'am Römerholz'. 1869. 66 × 92 cm. Signed lower right: Renoir.

A view in the same direction as the Moscow version (Plate 18), this picture looks out further into the river and shows more of the jetty leading to the round artificial island, which forms the centre of focus of the Stockholm picture (Plate II). It is as if, in these three paintings, the artist's eye is moving around the scene before him, scanning from the bank with its bathing huts, round towards the river, jetty and restaurant. The paint in this picture seems more oily and fluid than in the Moscow *La Grenouillère*, which has a much crustier paint texture; the figures again seem mostly to have been added at a second, later sitting or in the studio.

(*opposite*)
I *Portrait of Jules LeCoeur in the Forest of Fontainebleau*
SÃO PAULO, Museu de Arte. 106 × 80 cm. Signed and dated lower right: A Renoir 1866.

Although this picture was probably painted in Paris during the winter of 1865–66 when Renoir was sharing Sisley's studio, it was inspired by his work in the forest around Marlotte in the early summer of 1865. The village of Marlotte was near Barbizon, where painters had for many years sought quiet communion with nature and refuge from the pressures of nearby Parisian art life. Here many of them had settled, Théodore Rousseau in 1836, Diaz, Millet in 1849, and Jacque, painting the often eerie vistas of bulbous, primeval rocks, vast growths amid the ancient trees. It seems likely that the dark palette which Diaz criticized Renoir for using relates to landscape paintings earlier than this portrait, of which no examples survive, but which may have been influenced by the older Barbizon painters such as Rousseau, whose use of bitumen to produce deep transparent browns meant that his paint surfaces rapidly blackened and blistered, causing the original subtle effects to disappear. Renoir was friendly with Jules LeCoeur from about 1865 until 1874. This painting was rejected by the Salon jury of 1867.

20 *La Grenouillère*, detail of Plate II

The adjustment to the boat, left foreground, can be clearly seen here, as can the addition of the little group of bathing figures immediately above the jetty.

(opposite)
II *La Grenouillère*
STOCKHOLM, Nationalmuseum. 1869. 66 × 81 cm. Signed lower left: A Renoir.

The extent to which the artist is 'composing' can be seen in the lateness of his addition of the boat, foreground left; to the left of this boat another boat-shaped outline can be seen. It could be argued that here Renoir was changing the position of the boat because the boat before him had in fact moved. However, it is clear that the projected alignment of the boat would have tended to lead the eye out of the composition, while its present position, reinforced by the introduction of the small figure leaning over towards it, draws the eye around in a curve to the central group of figures. There is much evidence of *pentimenti* in the foreground. This painting should be compared with Monet's similar view (fig. 5), which shows a much crisper handling and more confidence in the rendering of texture; Renoir had not yet gained a comparable assurance in his *plein air* work. His handling is generally softer and more delicate than Monet's, with a less articulate sense of space and illusion of depth.

21 *La Grenouillère*, detail of Plate II

This high jetty, which presumably gave onto the restaurant at the right, is difficult to 'read' in Renoir's painting; the construction becomes evident on comparison with Monet's version (fig. 5). Renoir made the reflection of this jetty disturbingly strong, while the transition between foreground and distance here, following the water under the jetty to the boats in the background, is awkward and appears to make use of several different view-points. There is considerable reworking visible in this detail, apparent in the dry, old brushwork appearing under the paint surface of the jetty and boat.

22 *Portrait of Mme. Darras*
NEW YORK, Metropolitan Museum of Art (gift of Margaret Seligman Lewisohn, in memory of her husband, Samuel A. Lewisohn, and of her sister-in-law, Adele Lewisohn Lehman). 78·9 × 62·2 cm. Signed and dated lower right: A Renoir 71.

Cooper (1959) suggests that Renoir met Captain and Mme. Darras through his friends the LeCoeurs; his pendant portrait of Captain Darras is in the Staatliche Gemäldegalerie, Dresden. The superb treatment of textures and rich materials shows Renoir to have been more confident in his figure work than in landscape at this period. Renoir also painted an equestrian portrait of Mme. Darras (Plate 25).

24 *The Pont Neuf*
WASHINGTON, National Gallery of Art (Ailsa Mellon Bruce collection). 75 × 92 cm. Signed and dated lower left: A Renoir 72.

Renoir did not restrict his *plein air* studies to the countryside, but sought out suitable motifs in Paris too. This is one of the studies he did in 1872 of the Pont Neuf, his methods for which were recorded by his brother Edmond: 'We established our quarters at the entresol of a little café at a corner of the Quai du Louvre, but much nearer the Seine than are the present buildings. For two coffees, at ten centimes each, we could stay at that café for hours. From here Auguste dominated the bridge and took pleasure, after having outlined the soil, the parapets, the houses in the distance, the Place Dauphine and the statue of Henri IV, in sketching the passersby, vehicles and groups. Meanwhile I scribbled, except when he asked me to go on the bridge and speak with passersby to make them stop for a minute' (quoted by Rewald, 1945). Renoir thus had time to sketch the figures into his painting while they were delayed briefly by his brother enquiring the time or the whereabouts of a street with which he was doubtless quite familiar.

(*opposite*)
23 *Still-life with Bouquet*
HOUSTON, Museum of Fine Arts (gift of Mrs. Sarah Campbell Blaffer, Robert Lee Blaffer memorial collection). 75 × 58 cm. Signed and dated lower right: A Renoir 71.

This still-life includes a Japanese painted fan of the type popular in artistic circles in France and which were often depicted in the works of Renoir's contemporaries; Renoir and Monet both owned Japanese prints, which were an enormous influence at this period. Renoir seems to have been the least affected by the different conventions in Oriental art, however, retaining, as is implied by the image on the wall, stronger connections with the European tradition. On the wall Renoir depicted a print by Manet after his *Little Cavaliers*, a copy (Oslo, collection of Tryggve Sagan, 1855?) after a painting in the Louvre then attributed to Velázquez.

25 *Riding in the Bois de Boulogne*
HAMBURG, Kunsthalle. 261 × 226 cm. Signed and dated lower left: A Renoir 1873.

The sitters for this large scale portrait were Mme. Darras (see Plate 22) and the young Joseph LeCoeur. This was one of Renoir's two paintings rejected by the Salon jury of 1873 and shown at the special Salon des Refusés of that year. This picture is also called *The Amazon*.

(*opposite top*)
26 *The Seine at Argenteuil*
PORTLAND (OREGON), Portland Art Museum. c. 1873. 50 × 65·5 cm. Signed lower right: Renoir.

Although similar in technique to his studies of La Grenouillère, Renoir here showed a greater confidence and a relaxed atmosphere. This painting, also known as *Sailboats at Argenteuil*, should be compared to Monet's view of the same motif, reproduced in Rewald, 1973, p. 352.

(*opposite bottom*)
27 *The Seine at Argenteuil*
PARIS, Musée du Louvre. c. 1873. 46·5 × 65 cm. Signed lower right: Renoir.

This delicate, sweeping view of the Seine was obviously executed rapidly on the spot, with no apparent later additions. The atmospheric sensation of a warm, hazy day is accurately captured, while a sense of space is achieved through the diminishing scale of brushwork towards the horizon and the use of darker colours in the foreground.

49

(*top*)
28 *Argenteuil: The Harvesters*
ZÜRICH, private collection. 60 × 73·5 cm. Signed and dated lower left: Renoir 73.

This was one of Renoir's seven paintings, including *La Parisienne* (Plate 33) and *La Loge* (Plate 34), shown at the first Impressionist Exhibition held in the photographer Nadar's old studios, 35 boulevard des Capucines, from 15 April to 15 May 1874. In *Le Charivari*, Louis Leroy, who coined the name 'Impressionists', published an article on the show on 25 April, which, despite its hostility, showed a remarkable degree of understanding of Renoir's methods:

'So, M. Renoir is on the right track; there is nothing superfluous in his *Harvesters*. I even dare say his figures . . . are too overworked.'
'Oh, M. Vincent! But just look at these three touches of colour which are supposed to represent a man in the midst of wheat!' 'There are two too many; one would have been sufficient.'

(*opposite bottom*)
29 *The Gust of Wind*
CAMBRIDGE, Fitzwilliam Museum. c. 1873. 52 × 82·5 cm. Signed lower right: A Renoir.

Technically and stylistically, the *Fisher with Rod and Line* (Plate 30) and *The Gust of Wind* are both close to the dated *Harvesters,* indicating that these two undated works should be placed in 1873 or possibly 1874. This painting shows the rapid execution and sketchy finish of work done before the motif in a single sitting. While the oil sketch was widely popular among landscapists, even in official art circles interest in the use of the sketch technique had been increasing. An attempt to institutionalize the radical potential of and to incorporate what was valuable in both the oil sketch and landscape painting had been made as early as 1816, when the compositional sketch and a Prix de Rome for historical landscape were added to the list of competitions at the Ecole des Beaux-Arts.

(*above*)
30 *Fisher with Rod and Line* or *The Angler*
LONDON, private collection. 1873–74. 54 × 65 cm. Signed lower right: Renoir.

This canvas was among those sold at an auction arranged by Monet, Renoir, Sisley and Berthe Morisot at the Hôtel Drouot in March 1875 in a desperate attempt to raise funds for themselves. Morisot was the only one not then in need of money, but she loyally joined her friends in the venture. There was a general slump in the market during the mid-1870s, which did little to encourage buyers; of all the four, Renoir's works fetched the lowest prices, with an average of 112 francs. Amid the hostile furore that accompanied the sale, the *Fisher* was knocked down to Renoir's new patron Georges Charpentier for 180 francs.

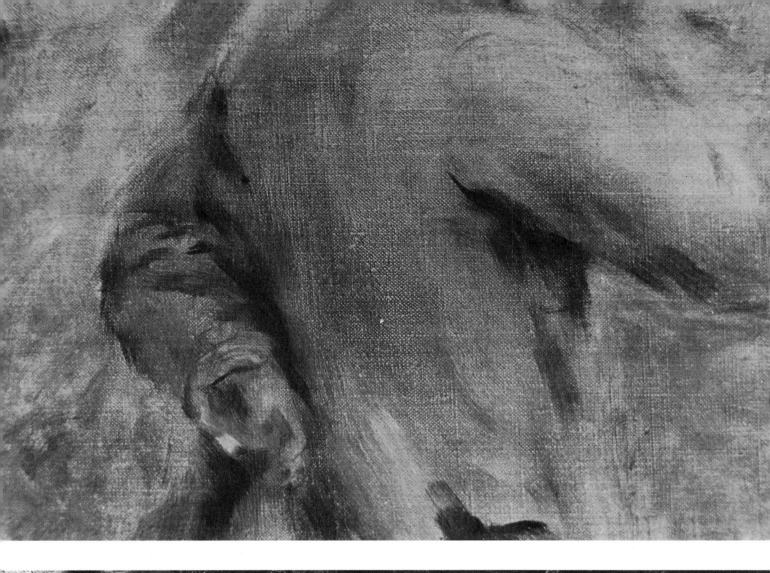

33 *La Parisienne*
CARDIFF, National Museum of Wales (Gwendoline E. Davies collection). 160 × 106 cm. Signed and dated lower left: A Renoir 74.

At the first Impressionist Exhibition of 1874, *La Parisienne* was sold to Renoir's fellow artist and exhibitor Henri Rouart. When Paul Signac visited Rouart's collection on 16 February 1898 he recorded in his diary: 'I saw so much that I left feeling overwhelmed. My clearest memories are of a Delacroix sketch . . . and of a large portrait of a woman in blue by Renoir of 1874. The dress is blue, an intense and pure blue which, by contrast, makes the flesh yellow, and, by its reflection, green. The tricks of colour are admirably recorded. And it is simple, it is beautiful, and it is fresh. One would think that this picture painted twenty years ago had only left the studio today' (quoted in Ingamells). Renoir represented here a working-class Parisian girl as opposed to a highly fashionable sophisticated woman. He always preferred the simple coquettish appeal of young milliners and seamstresses, perhaps feeling more at home in their company, as his own rather gauche manners meant he was often ill-at-ease in more elegant surroundings. In practical terms, apart from friends, portrait sitters and professional models, working girls would have been the only models available to him.

(*opposite top*)
31 *Fisher with Rod and Line*, detail of Plate 30

In this detail of the back of the angler, the fairly fine but irregular weave of the canvas is clearly visible beneath a thin, commercial oil ground of pale beige. Renoir's method of rubbing away a delicate wash of paint is shown here, leaving only a minimal veil of oil colour to give a sense of form in the figure with the coloured ground playing an active rôle. Dark and light accents were then added in more saturated, more opaque colour and fluid, rapid brushstrokes.

(*opposite bottom*)
32 *Fisher with Rod and Line*, detail of Plate 30

A darker green lay-in over the pale ground here forms the basis of a predominantly darker area in this detail of foliage, river and the upper-right far bank. Over this colour foundation, which evokes the water surface, Renoir used contrasting touches of impasto to give the sense of moving foliage above the water, and the opposite bank and its reflection, which were themselves produced by longer, broader strokes of paint. An occasional slim, long vertical brushstroke effectively suggests the stems of the foreground bushes (cf. entire picture, Plate 30), although here in the detail, appearing more abstract, their function does not make complete visual sense. Touches of both dark and light impasto of viridian, ultramarine and flake white are in evidence; the dark touches form both foliage and shadows, while the light dabs describe the palest parts of the plants and also the highlights on the water. It is clear that many of the impasted strokes of light pigment were here worked directly into, bleeding into, the dark impastoes, emphasizing the speed of execution in this painting.

34 La Loge
LONDON, Courtauld Institute Galleries. 80 × 64 cm. Signed and dated lower left: A Renoir 74.

La Loge was shown at the first Impressionist Exhibition of 1874. Renoir afterwards persuaded the dealer Père Martin to buy it for 425 francs which he desperately needed for his rent. This superb study of modern life was posed by Renoir's younger brother Edmond and a new model called Nini. A smaller version of this painting was sold at the 1875 sale.

(opposite)
35 La Loge, detail of Plate 34

The paint here is remarkably thin and delicate, with touches of impasto highlighting the pearls and the fine pattern of lace at the sitter's neckline. The palette is rich and sonorous, focusing strong light-dark contrasts on the main female figure.

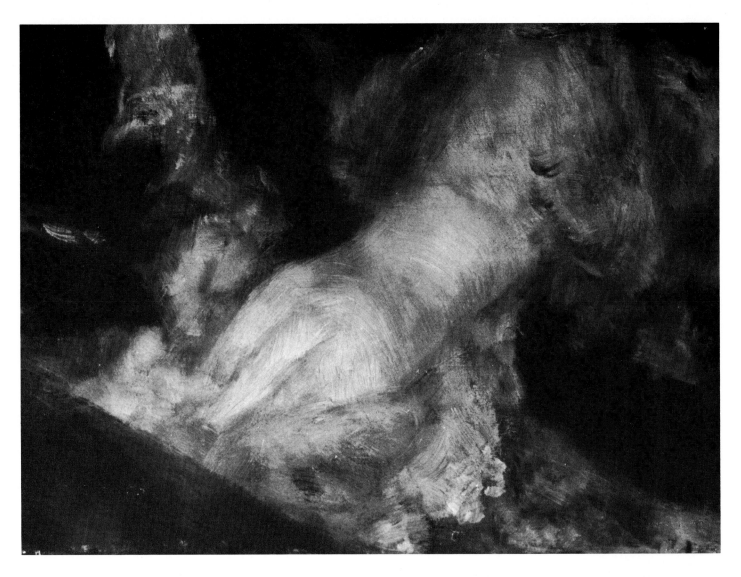

36 *La Loge*, detail of Plate 34

Similarly the paint on this section of the canvas is again thin, despite the sense of impasto in the highlights. Detail was brushed in loosely and without definition, and the paint quality is dry and pastel-like. The particular thinness of the paint may be the result of some sinking of the colour with age, which is common in oil paints.

37 *La Liseuse*

PARIS, Musée du Louvre. 1875–76. 46·5 × 38·5 cm. Signed centre left: Renoir.

La Liseuse is a painting from the **Gustave Caillebotte** collection. Renoir here avoided all use of black, which sometimes appears in his portraits of the 1870s, and instead, viridian green and French ultramarine provide the darkest notes, while touches of vermilion and a variety of yellows in her hair, face and ruffle are countered by touches of this green and blue mixture, lightened with white and probably some cobalt blue. Thus warm and cool contrasts are strongly and vividly in evidence here. Both in subject type and in Renoir's delicate paint handling, this study evokes the work of Fragonard and again emphasizes Renoir's debt to eighteenth-century French painting.

38 *Claude Monet Painting in his Garden at Argenteuil*
HARTFORD, Wadsworth Atheneum. c. 1874. 50 × 106 cm. Signed lower left: A Renoir.

Renoir painted this picture while both he and Monet were working together in Monet's garden at
Argenteuil; Rewald (1973) identifies a painting on which Monet may have been working while
Renoir painted his portrait and suggests a date of 1873 for the portrait. The more heavily worked
and impasted surface here, with small dabs of paint and a more uniform brushwork may suggest a
slightly later date, compared to his technique in dated paintings of 1873 (e.g. Plate 28). In this
portrait Renoir showed the height and position of Monet's canvas arranged so that he could look
over and to the right of it towards his chosen motif. Working on a subject to the right of artist and
canvas is the most comfortable choice for a right-handed painter. Evidence of underwork in this
painting, such as between Monet's legs and those of the easel, indicates that here again Renoir was
probably re-using an old canvas.

(above left)
39 Portrait of Mme. Victor Chocquet
STUTTGART, Staatsgalerie. 75 × 60 cm. Signed and dated centre right: Renoir 75.

This was the first of several portraits of Chocquet's wife that Renoir was commissioned to paint. In the background here and in the portrait of Chocquet himself (Plate 40) Renoir included at Chocquet's request two of his oil studies by Delacroix for the Palais Bourbon decorations. As can be seen here in the background left, through the open door beside Mme. Chocquet's right arm, Chocquet was also an avid collector of antique furniture and *objets d'art*.

(above right)
40 Portrait of Victor Chocquet
CAMBRIDGE (MASSACHUSETTS), Fogg Art Museum (bequest of Grenville L. Winthrop). 1875. 47 × 37 cm. Signed lower left: Renoir.

Probably painted in the same year as the *Portrait of Mme. Victor Chocquet* (Plate 39), this portrait shows Renoir using a structured network of small, often impasted brushstrokes, building up a delicate rhythm of hatching across the surface of the picture. Renoir placed his sitter in a very shallow pictorial space where the close proximity of the background projects his subject towards us. He set Chocquet's entwined hands diagonally across the bottom left to act as a compositional device situating the figure behind the picture plane. In his 1877 portrait of Chocquet (Columbus, Ohio, Columbus Gallery of Fine Arts), Cézanne adopted Renoir's pose, reversing the position of the hands. Renoir did not hesitate here to distort the frame on the Delacroix study in the background in order to achieve the required compositional structure. This seems an extremely sensitive portrait of a person Renoir liked and admired and a person who he felt confident would enjoy the painting.

(opposite)
III Portrait of Mme. Monet
WILLIAMSTOWN, Sterling and Francine Clark Art Institute. 1872. 61·2 × 50·3 cm. Signed lower left: A Renoir.

This delicious study of Mme. Monet, taken from an almost direct front view which tilts the sitter upright and brings the whole image close to the picture plane, is painted in very thin, light touches of paint. The canvas grain is visible over almost the entire surface, and the pale ground frequently shows through among the loose brushstrokes. The *Portrait of Mme. Darras* (Plate 22) appears quite conventional beside this picture, where there was no necessity to please the sitter, and Renoir was therefore free to experiment. The brushwork here achieved a greater uniformity of touch, rather than using a more 'finished' technique for the flesh areas. Three Japanese fans were included on the wall behind the sitter.

41 *Woman's Torso in Sunlight,* detail of Plate IV

As this detail demonstrates, Renoir never completely treated the human figure as if it were of no more importance than landscape. This painting is frequently used as an example of the artist's preoccupation with the effects of sunlight at this period, yet his concern with the form of the figure is still evident; in this detail and on the right of the figure, the grass is depicted only cursorily and the pale ground is still clearly visible. The brushwork on the figure, however, although broad is carefully controlled, and the paint is more densely built up. While the patches of light on the form do create a separate surface pattern, they do not entirely erode the solidity of the figure. A series of fine, individual, hatched brushstrokes accentuate the warm shadow and the form of the underside of the breast here, worked in over the patch of colour representing the reflected sunlight.

(opposite)
IV *Woman's Torso in Sunlight*
PARIS, Musée du Louvre. 1875–76. 81 × 64·8 cm. Signed lower right: Renoir.

This painting was shown at the second Impressionist Exhibition of 1876, held at 11 rue Le Peletier in April. It was acquired by the group's friend and patron, the amateur painter Gustave Caillebotte, whose collection was left to the state in 1896 and caused such heated dispute that many of the works were refused.

42 *The Swing*
PARIS, Musée du Louvre. 92 × 73 cm. Signed and dated lower right: Renoir 76.

Both *The Swing* and *Dancing at The Moulin de la Galette* (Plate 43) belonged to Gustave Caillebotte
and were shown at the third Impressionist Exhibition of 1877, at 6 rue Le Peletier.

43 *Dancing at The Moulin de la Galette*
PARIS, Musée du Louvre. 130 × 175 cm. Signed and dated lower right: Renoir 76.

This is a typical scene of modern life, showing all the gaiety of the famous Parisian open-air dance hall where the rumbustious can-can originated: 'A wooden barrier separated the dance floor from the rough wooden tables where the customers drank the speciality of the house: pitchers of mulled wine. It was certainly not a "respectable" establishment, being an authentic working-class haunt with a public largely composed of working girls and working men on a spree together with an assortment of pimps, prostitutes, petty thieves and local toughs . . . Sundays, however, the Moulin de la Galette had a more innocent air of festivity as young apprentices, white collar employees and their sweethearts came up to the Butte for a sample of popular pleasures and a pleasurable suggestion of low life' (Rudorf). Renoir's painting captured the Sunday view of The Moulin, with female models chosen from among the girls who came to dance there. Among the male figures here are Renoir's friends Franc-Lamy, Goeneutte, Cordey, Rivière, Gervex, Lestringuez and Lhote.
Some of the critics seemed to understand more fully Renoir's aims when he showed this painting in 1877; the critic Charles O'Squarr wrote in the *Courrier de France*: 'A full, brutal light falls from the sky through the green transparencies of the foliage, gilding the blond hair and rosy cheeks, putting sparkles on the young girls' ribbons, illuminating all the background of the painting with a joyous flame which gives even the shadows a reflected light' (*Centenaire*). Chocquet owned a smaller version of this painting, and it is possible that he commissioned it after seeing this one which would have been too big for his crowded apartment; the smaller version (New York, collection of Mr. and Mrs. John Hay Whitney) is also dated 1876.

(*overleaf*)
44 *Dancing at The Moulin de la Galette*, detail of Plate 43

Here Renoir's Impressionist brushwork can be seen to advantage, deft, rhythmic touches picking up light and colour among the moving figures and creating a vivid impression of lively activity. It is interesting to note the overhead gas-lamps used to light the evening's entertainment before the invention of the electric light. Many artists did not use their studios after dark as the colour of artificial light was so different to daylight.

45 *The End of the Lunch*
FRANKFURT, Städelsches Kunstinstitut. 99·5 × 82 cm. Signed and dated lower left: Renoir 79.

The grouping of the figures here, with the man cut off at the right edge of the canvas, has a spontaneous quality about it, reminiscent of the arbitrariness of the photograph; it serves to place the compositional emphasis on the two female figures and to stop the eye from moving off the right side of the picture.

(*above left*)
46 *Two Little Circus Girls*
CHICAGO, Art Institute of Chicago (Potter Palmer collection). 1879. 130·9 × 98·5 cm. Signed lower left: Renoir.

These two girls were part of the Cirque Fernando which was set up on the boulevard Rochechouart in 1875. This painting was shown at the first exhibition of Impressionist paintings in New York in 1886, organized by Paul Durand-Ruel.

(*above right*)
47 *Portrait of Margot Bérard*
NEW YORK, Metropolitan Museum of Art (bequest of Stephen C. Clark). 41 × 32·4 cm. Signed and dated upper left: Renoir 79.

Marguerite Bérard, who was called Margot by her family, was the daughter of Renoir's patron Paul Bérard, a discriminating collector of Impressionist works who held an important position in the French diplomatic corps. Renoir became friendly with the Bérard family through the Charpentiers in 1879, and he visited their seaside home at Wargemont, near Dieppe, regularly from that date. This portrait, *The Children's Afternoon at Wargemont* (Plate 60) and the *Still-life with Peaches* (Plate 54) were all executed at Wargemont. The *Portrait of Margot Bérard* was shown at the third annual exhibition of Les XX in Brussels in 1886.

48 *Mme. Charpentier and her Children*
NEW YORK, Metropolitan Museum of Art (Wolfe fund). 153·7 × 190·2 cm. Signed and dated lower right: Renoir 78.

As the Metropolitan Museum catalogue points out, this family portrait shows not the two Charpentier daughters but the son Paul, aged three, beside his mother, and the eldest child, six-year-old Georgette, on the back of their dog Porto. The second daughter, Jeanne, was not born until 1880, two years after this painting was executed. The catalogue also states, 'Several critics have commented on colour changes in the picture, but a cleaning has restored all its original brilliance.' Up to forty sittings were reported to have been required for this important commission, which was set in the family's Japanese drawing room in their mansion on the rue de Grenelle. Edmond Renoir reported that nothing was rearranged for the portrait.

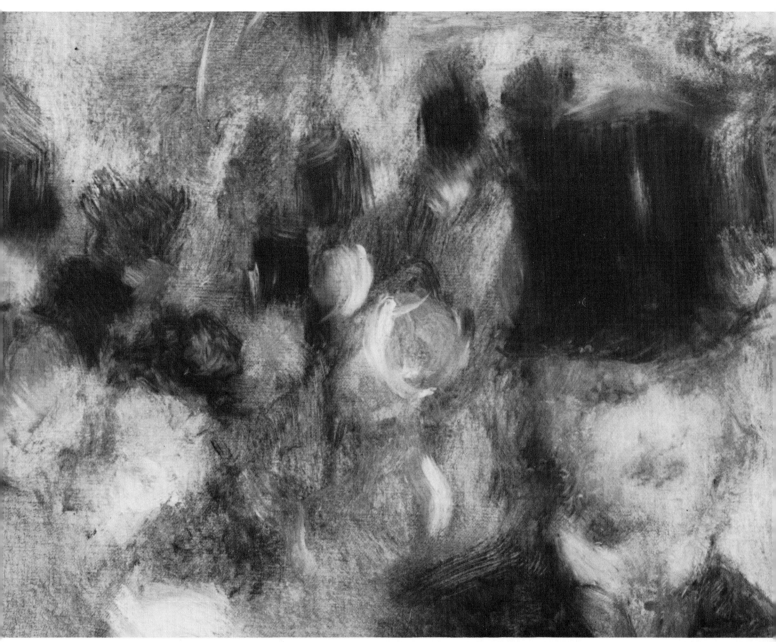

50 *Place Clichy*, detail of Plate 49

Renoir's technique of rubbing away dark lay-in colours over a light ground is visible here in the bottom left-hand corner and elsewhere under later touches. He modulated his removal of the colour allowing greater amounts to remain where he needed to indicate shadow and around the edge of figures, thus modelling form simply and effectively.

(opposite)
49 *Place Clichy*
Private collection. c. 1880. 64·5 × 54·5 cm. Signed lower left: A Renoir.

Often mistitled 'Place Pigalle', this painting shows Renoir again returning to the theme of the city, but here concentrating on the busy movement of figures on the street to the almost total exclusion of the architecture. Technically, this painting relates to his *Fisher with Rod and Line* of 1873–74 (Plate 30), in its use of rubbed colour. Although the cut-off figure of the woman in the foreground was painted with distinctly different brushwork to any to be found in the *Fisher with Rod and Line*—in *Place Clichy* Renoir used a much more controlled and directional, fine stroke for his key figure—the unfocused jostle of figures in the background was scumbled in lightly, and in places the paint has been rubbed away, leaving only a slight colouration which deepens at the edges, for example in the figure immediately next to the woman's face (see detail, Plate 50). Renoir here exploited a white rather than a coloured ground to obtain maximum luminosity and increase the transparency of his colours; as in his earlier landscapes, he again obtained transparent darks through the mixture of transparent pigments, ultramarine and rose madder.

52 *Field of Banana Trees*
PARIS, Musée du Louvre. 51·5 × 63·5 cm. Signed and dated lower left: Renoir 1881.

This painting was executed during Renoir's first trip to Algeria in the spring of 1881; it was shown by Durand-Ruel at the seventh group show of 1882 against Renoir's wishes—he refused to be associated with newcomers like Gauguin—and told his dealer to exhibit paintings owned by him, making clear that it was not Renoir who chose to exhibit. Eugène Manet wrote to his wife, Berthe Morisot, on 1 March 1882 concerning the show and commenting on this painting: 'A landscape of palm-trees, highly successful', mistaking the bananas for palms (quoted by Rouart).

(*opposite*)
51 *At the Concert*
WILLIAMSTOWN, Sterling and Francine Clark Art Institute. 1880. 99 × 80·6 cm. Signed centre left: Renoir.

The gentle sensuality of these two figures, accentuated by luxuriant materials and dark surroundings, is even more marked than in Renoir's earlier *La Loge* (Plate 34). The contemporary predilection for the hair as a vehicle for sensual delight, second only to the *décolletage* as a feast for the eye, was exploited here by Renoir; his extension of the girl's tresses over her pale dress is particularly noticeable where the dark paint cuts across earlier dry colour. He may also have covered more of the light dress area for compositional reasons: a greater expanse of highlight would have placed too much emphasis on the right-hand figure. This adjustment may have taken place after Renoir painted out the male figure which he originally included standing behind the women.

53 *Luncheon of the Boating Party*
WASHINGTON, Phillips Collection. 130 × 175·5 cm. Signed and dated lower right: Renoir 1881.

Painted at the popular restaurant Fournaise on the island of Chatou, this painting is in the same genre as *Dancing at The Moulin de la Galette* (Plate 43), with its crowd of Sunday pleasure-seekers relaxing over a long lunch. Again many of Renoir's friends posed for him, including to the left Aline Charigot, whom the artist married in 1890. In the right foreground is Gustave Caillebotte, sitting beside Angèle, a model of Renoir; leaning over them is the young Fournaise, son of the proprietor, while at the back are the critic Charles Ephrussi in a top hat, Lestringuez in a bowler, and Lhote in a straw hat. The *Luncheon* was shown at the seventh group show of 1882, where Eugène Manet commented: 'The painting of the boating party by Renoir looks very good' (quoted by Rouart).

(opposite top)
54 *Still-life with Peaches*
NEW YORK, Metropolitan Museum of Art (bequest of Stephen C. Clark). 53·3 × 64·7 cm. Signed and dated lower right: Renoir 81.

According to Paul Bérard, this jardinière, probably of delftware, was a frequent decoration on the dining table at the family house at Wargemont, where Renoir undoubtedly painted both this still-life and another version, with grapes, also in the Metropolitan Museum. The white ground in this painting is very dense, obscuring all the canvas grain except at the edges, providing a surface which seems similar to that in *The Return from the Fields* (Plate 67). On this smooth ground Renoir laid his colours in thin transparent washes, each brushstroke remaining intact. The beginnings of a more structured hatched brushstroke are visible, particularly in the ornamental screen or wallpaper decorating the background. Renoir was in Wargemont in July 1881.

55 *Still-life with Onions*
WILLIAMSTOWN, Sterling and Francine Clark Art Institute. 39·1 × 60·6 cm. Signed and dated lower left and inscribed: Renoir Naples 81.

This fabulous still-life was evidently one of the paintings completed during Renoir's stay in Naples. The solidity of the shapes is achieved by subtle colour gradation and parallel small brushstrokes which echo the turn of the form while evoking the ridged onion flesh. The ground here is again thick, giving a mainly smooth, untextured surface.

(*above left*)
56 *Venice: The Doge's Palace*
WILLIAMSTOWN, Sterling and Francine Clark Art Institute. 54·3 × 65·3 cm. Signed and dated lower right: Renoir 81.

Venice was Renoir's first stop on his visit to Italy in the autumn and winter of 1881–82; in the autumn he wrote to the collector Charles Deudon: 'I have done the Doge's Palace viewed from Saint-Georges opposite, I don't think it had been done before. There were at least six of us in the queue!' (quoted by White). Renoir also told him that a colour merchant would be forwarding this and another study to his Paris studio when they were drier, within a fortnight. As Renoir mentioned elsewhere that he had 'indispensible retouches' to do on his Italian paintings, it seems likely that *The Doge's Palace* was no exception; this seems confirmed by the fact that the signature and date were obviously painted on separate occasions, the date probably being added after the artist's return to Paris, when retouching was complete. According to Eugène Manet more than one 'detestable' view of Venice was on show in March, and as the artist did not return to Paris until after the end of April 1882, this must have been before any retouching took place, if this was one of the views shown.

(*above right*)
57 *Vesuvius: The Port of Naples*
WILLIAMSTOWN, Sterling and Francine Clark Art Institute. 56·5 × 79 cm. Signed and dated lower left: Renoir 81.

Renoir was not alone in concentrating on painting famous tourist scenes; Monet regularly chose such popular motifs in France in the hope of attracting buyers.

(*opposite*)
58 *Blond Bather*
WILLIAMSTOWN, Sterling and Francine Clark Art Institute. 81·8 × 65·7 cm. Signed and dated upper right and inscribed: à M. H. Vever. Renoir 81; [painted out] Renoir 81.

Blond Bather was the first major figure composition in Renoir's new so-called 'harsh' style. He depicted a pale-complexioned, though buxom beauty; this is in contrast to his work of the 1870s, where his nudes are rosy-cheeked and suntanned and to his later paintings of ordinary healthy country girls (Plate IX). The often pallid skins of his figures of the 1880s may have reflected the contemporary fashion for white 'aesthetic' skins, a notion imported from England, the Pre-Raphaelites and Swinburne: 'Their ideal woman had the lines of the lily, she had its pallor and, to hostile critics, no more sex appeal than the flower. In France, as in England, the lily came to be the symbol of *fin de siècle* preciosity' (Rudorf). While their skins do have something of this 'Decadent' paleness, Renoir's nudes could hardly be accused of having proportions to match; thus, if fashionable, they are also contradictorily robust and healthy in appearance. It should also be noticed that Renoir gave his nude a wedding ring; in fact few of his nudes are without one and he often seems to contrive a pose to expose a ringed left hand (Plates 15, IV, 69, 87). This may have reflected Renoir's conservative nature, although he did not marry his mistress Aline till ten years after they met, but more likely it was done with an eye to conservative buyers.

59 *Cradle Rock, Guernsey*
LONDON, National Gallery. 1883. 29·1 × 54 cm. Signed lower left: Renoir.

Of the Guernsey beach scenes Renoir wrote to Durand-Ruel in September 1883: 'One would
think oneself much more in a Watteau landscape than in reality' (quoted in Venturi, vol. I).
This was the sort of 'on-the-motif' sketch that he referred to as 'documents', and which he used in
his Paris studio on his return as material for composed pictures such as *By the Seashore* (Plate 65).
This sketch must have been executed in a single sitting, as even the little foreground figures were
worked into wet paint. The ground Renoir used here is cream, while the palette is reminiscent of
works of ten years earlier such as *The Gust of Wind* (Plate 29), except here it is hotter and more
scintillating. Ultramarine and rose madder are used extensively to create the shadows on the rocks,
while the sea is predominantly composed of an emerald green and flake white mixture.

(*opposite*)
V *The Skiff*
LONDON, private collection. c. 1879. 71 × 92 cm. Signed lower left: Renoir.

This is a delicious interpretation of the softening, hazy effects of summer sun, dissolving the
distance and flickering brilliantly off the surface of the moving water. The brushwork varies from
one texture to another, thin and frond-like for the reeds in the foreground, dry and short for the
water, soft and limpid in the background. The bright blues of the water are heightened by the
contrasting reflections of warm orange from the skiff.

60 *The Children's Afternoon at Wargemont*
BERLIN, Staatliche Gemäldegalerie. 127 × 173 cm. Signed and dated . . . [unclear]: Renoir 84.

This painting, which contains all the precision and cool calm of Renoir's Ingresque style of the mid-1880s, has a haunting stillness and naïvety, accentuated by the lack of shadows and the gravity of the poses. Paul Bérard's three daughters are portrayed here, from left to right: Marguerite (see Plate 47), Lucie and Marthe, aged respectively, ten, four and fourteen years old.

(*opposite top*)
VI *Mosque at Algiers*
PARIS, collection of Stavros S. Niarchos. 49 × 60 cm. Signed and dated lower right: Renoir 82.

By the end of January 1882 Renoir had left Italy and joined Cézanne for a period of work together at L'Estaque. Following a bout of serious illness there, Renoir left on 10 March for a second, longer visit to Algeria. The *Mosque,* which is an excellent example of the artist's ability to create a breathing sense of sunlight and warmth, was again painted on a thick white ground which reveals no canvas grain. A heavy impasto was employed in the areas of highlight, while the darker sections used delicate strokes of wash-like colour.

(*opposite bottom*)
VII *Algerian Landscape: The Ravine of 'La Femme Sauvage'*
PARIS, Musée du Louvre. 1881. 65·5 × 81 cm. Signed lower left: Renoir.

Another of his 1881 Algerian landscapes, *The Ravine* was executed in a rich, colourful palette and often crusted impasto; there are areas of contrasting dense opaque colour mixed with flake white and transparent touches of madder and viridian. Accents of vermilion and emerald green further enliven this vivid paint surface.

62 *The Daughters of Paul Durand-Ruel*, detail of Plate 61

The relaxed and harmonious atmosphere of this painting compares favourably with the more static, posed scene in *The End of the Lunch* (Plate 45). This detail shows how Renoir translated the effects of dappled sunlight without losing the form of the faces; the dabs of paint highlighting the sun on the leaves and the strong rendering of reflected light on the figures produce a unity close to, but more successful than, that of *The Swing* (Plate 42), and by contrast to his later outdoor figure work of the 1880s.

(*opposite*)
61   *The Daughters of Paul Durand-Ruel*
NORFOLK (VIRGINIA), Chrysler Museum. 81 × 65 cm. Signed and dated lower right: Renoir 82.

Renoir painted several portraits of his dealer, Paul Durand-Ruel, and his family, including one of his sons Charles and Georges (Paris, Durand-Ruel collection), painted in almost the same setting as that of this portrait and in the same year. This painting was done during August of 1882, and Renoir achieved a high degree of harmony between the two girls and the surrounding foliage; the treatment of sunlight falling through the leaves onto the sitters and the soft feathery brushwork in the foreground are both unifying factors.

64 *Dance at Bougival*
BOSTON, Museum of Fine Arts. 180 × 98 cm. Signed and
dated lower right: Renoir 83.

Renoir painted three different versions of the *Dance*; this
one was begun in the autumn of 1882 but not finished
until the following year. In addition there is the *Dance in
the Country* (Paris, private collection, 1883) and the contrasting *Dance in the Town* (Paris, private collection, 1883).
They show the comparative dress, manners and setting of
country and town, the latter producing an image of cool,
elegant restraint in composition, choice of interior location
and palette, by contrast to the enthusiastic warmth of the
two outdoor country versions. While the figure of the
dancing girl, particularly in the treatment of the face,
shows something of Renoir's new concern for classicizing
purity, overall the technique is reminiscent of his *Luncheon
of the Boating Party* (Plate 53) of two years earlier, and the
softly painted group of drinkers in the background harks
back to the foreground figures in *Dancing at The Moulin de
la Galette* (Plate 43). However, in the foliage there is
evidence of Renoir's search for a more structured paint
surface in the Cézannesque diagonal hatched brushstrokes.
Renoir's delicious feel for detail is here shown in the
inclusion of casually stubbed cigarette butts and spent
matches which litter the rough earth of the dance floor
and which also help to locate the plane of the floor in the
pictorial space. This steep angle of the floor accentuates
the importance of the two central figures, pushing them
out towards the spectator, while their upper surroundings
draw them into the lively scene behind. The couple who
posed for this picture were Renoir's brother Edmond and
Suzanne Valadon, whose self-portrait of 1915 (fig. 9)
provides an interesting comparison with Renoir's softened
idealization of her features. *Dance at Bougival* was exhibited
in London between April and July of 1883, having been
shipped there by Renoir's dealer as soon as it was complete. Durand-Ruel was again trying to popularize the
work of the Impressionists by organizing this large
exhibition of their work at Dowdeswell's Galleries in New
Bond Street; he had given up his own London premises
in the mid-1870s because of financial pressures.

(opposite)
63 *The Umbrellas*
LONDON, National Gallery. 1881/2–85/6. 180 × 115 cm. Signed lower right: Renoir.

This painting typifies the stylistic change which Renoir's work underwent in the early 1880s, the
figures on the right having been painted in a predominantly Impressionist manner, while the girl
with the bandbox on the left is an example of his 'harsh' style of the mid-1880s. As Martin Davies
pointed out: 'The two little girls and to some extent the lady behind them are in an earlier style
than the girl with the band-box; it is clear that Renoir worked on [this painting] over some years.
The material condition of the picture . . . confirms that there was an extensive re-casting. It is not
excluded that Renoir did some retouching to the earlier parts when completing it. The dates can
be established fairly accurately from the costume, 1881/2 for the earlier part, 1885/6 for the girl
with the band-box, if the figures are not dressed noticeably behind the fashion.' It is evident that
this picture gave Renoir problems, causing him to set it aside for several years and then later to
alter the overall canvas format by several inches, at the same time reworking the composition and
repainting major areas in his new style.

65 *By the Seashore*
NEW YORK, Metropolitan Museum of Art (H. O. Havemeyer collection). 92·1 × 72·4 cm. Signed and dated lower left: Renoir 83.

By the Seashore was probably painted in the late autumn of 1883 after Renoir's return from Guernsey. There are several patches of white ground and canvas grain showing through the paint, particularly along the bottom edge; elsewhere the canvas grain is not much in evidence and may have been obliterated by the ground. The relationship between figure and background is unusual, strengthening the argument that this is a studio picture; *By the Seashore* can be compared to *The Daughters of Paul Durand-Ruel* (Plate 61), where the figures and setting achieve a natural integration.

66 *By the Seashore*, detail of Plate 65

The brushwork of the face and hat can be contrasted with the looser, more sketchy treatment of the landscape behind. There is evidently a patch of *pentimenti* rising through the final paint-layer at the back of the girl's neck; perhaps Renoir originally intended to give her long hair or braids.

69 *Bather Arranging her Hair*
WILLIAMSTOWN, Sterling and Francine Clark Art Institute.
91·9 × 73 cm. Signed and dated lower left: Renoir 85.

This painting is built up of impasted strokes of rich
undiluted pigment, often mixed with flake white to
increase the opacity. It shows evidence of a dragging of
the dryish paint across the surface, leaving darker speckles
relating to the canvas grain beneath, for example, along
the contour of the nude's shoulder and raised arm and in
the sea and horizon lines. The flesh is almost sculpted in
the thick layer of smoother paint, and shadows are
virtually non-existent; as in the *Blond Bather* (Plate 58) of
four years earlier, the sense of form depends largely on
the strength of the contour. This is emphasized by the
brushwork in the landscape immediately surrounding the
bather, which mostly follows the shape of the figure
rather than the diagonal hatchings of the landscape and
sea. The exaggerated brushwork around the extended right
elbow may be the result of *pentimenti* caused by adjusting
the position of the arm.

(opposite top)
67 *The Return from the Fields*
CAMBRIDGE, Fitzwilliam Museum. c. 1886. 54 × 65 cm. Signed lower right: Renoir.

This painting dates from Renoir's trip to Brittany in the late summer and autumn of 1886, when
he stayed at Saint-Briac for two months. A more finished version of this painting, in smaller
dimensions, is in a private collection in New York (see Daulte, 1971, no. 499); in it the woman and
cow are brought closer to the spectator than they appear in the Cambridge picture. This painting
is also called *The Woman, the Cow and the Ewe*.

(opposite bottom)
68 *The Return from the Fields,* detail of Plate 67

The artist's careful preparatory drawing can be seen in this detail, particularly in the adjustments
to the position of the sheep's front leg; less visible in this reproduction is the under-drawing of the
sheep's wool, where each curl received individual attention, the pencil indenting the thick ground.
This drawing, which Renoir used to tighten up the form and composition, was then translated into
brushstrokes of colour, creating a decorative, stylized surface structure. This type of preparatory
drawing, either in pencil or in pen and black ink, is a common feature in Renoir's oils of this
period and is most easily seen in his less finished works. Near the corner of the canvas here, the
second white ground laid by the palette knife falls noticeably short of the extremities of the canvas,
revealing its rather haphazard preparation. In this painting Renoir used a subtle blend of earth
colours washed so thinly that they vibrate transparently over the dense white ground.

(*above left*)
70 *Woman Arranging her Hair*
LONDON, Lefevre Gallery. c. 1885. Pen and ink on paper. 42·5 × 25·5 cm. Signed lower right: Renoir.

Although recently dated to c. 1875, it seems likely that this drawing was done nearer in time to the painting to which it relates, *The Toilette* (Tokyo, Fuji International Art, 1885). In addition a dating to the mid-1870s is stylistically inaccurate, as Renoir here used a technique which permitted him to concentrate on the linear aspects of his form, stressing contour to the same degree as in his paintings of this period. The major alteration here between drawing and painting is the lowering of the chemise in the oil to reveal her left breast, producing a more relaxedly sensual image.

(*above right*)
71 *Study for 'The Large Bathers'*
CHICAGO, Art Institute of Chicago (gift of Kate L. Brewster). 1884–85. Pencil, black, red and white chalks and wash on pinkish paper. 98·5 × 64 cm. Unsigned.

This is one of Renoir's many preparatory drawings for his major painting of the 1880s, *The Large Bathers* (Plate 72). Again the modelling of form is reduced to a minimum, relying on the contour for solidity; Renoir here exploited the warm tone of the paper to enhance the flesh colour, and he surrounded the figure in white chalk to bring it up from the background. A comparison with the final painting will show the adjustments made to this figure, but it remains close to this large-scale, early conception.

72 *The Large Bathers*

PHILADELPHIA, Philadelphia Museum of Art (Mr. and Mrs. Carroll S. Tyson collection). 1884–87.
115 × 170 cm. Signed lower left: Renoir.

In addition to the inspiration of Girardon (fig. 10), Renoir had in mind here a low-relief series by
the French Renaissance sculptor Jean Goujon which he had discovered in his youth on the
Fontaine des Innocents in Les Halles, close to his childhood home. The static simplicity of these
figures is reminiscent of Ingres, whom Renoir always admired (fig. 8). The brushwork on the
figures is smoothed, unlike his nudes of the 1870s (Plate IV), and the awkward relationship between
figures and setting emphasizes that this was a studio composition. The head of the central bather,
top, should be compared with the head in the detail of *The Daughters of Paul Durand-Ruel* (Plates 61
and 62), where the relationship between figures and foliage was studied outdoors and shows a much
greater degree of naturalism. In *The Large Bathers* the brushwork is more tightly controlled, and the
depiction of the foliage more stylized and decorative. The small cracks in the paint surface amongst
the foliage are probably due either to heavier working in that area or to the use of lean paint
which dries quickly, over a fattier layer which dries more slowly, thus causing the top layer to
crack.

73 *Young Woman with a Swan*
UNITED STATES OF AMERICA, private collection. c. 1886. 76 × 62 cm. Signed upper right: Renoir.

This extraordinary painting, with its Ingresque rendering of the face contrasting with vigorous parallel brushwork elsewhere, was executed in a harsh range of predominantly yellow colours, which are picked up and reflected by the whitish dress. The unfocused, melancholy mien of the girl is a rare phenomenon in Renoir's usually light-hearted work. The almost mask-like quality of this face, particularly when compared to the highly vigorous hatched brushwork around it and to the very different treatment of the arms and hands, has a sculpted, death-like blandness. Not only

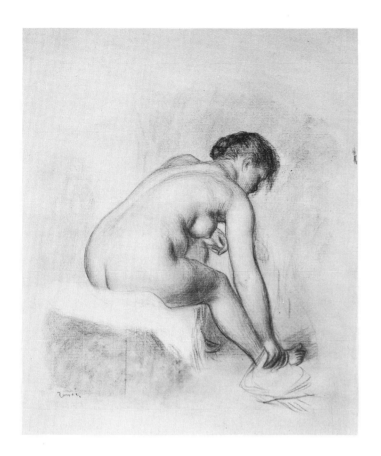 

is the brushwork on it different, it is also in a higher tonal key than the surrounding areas, which makes the face stand forward as a separate entity. In traditional iconographic terms this subject links with the mythological story of Leda and the swan. Several of Renoir's paintings from the mid-1880s have an unearthly, eerie mystery about them and seem prophetic of the moody Symbolism Gauguin later created. The impact of literary Symbolism on painting and the growing conflict between the ideologies of naturalism and idealism were among the chief sources of self-doubt among the older generation of Impressionists in the 1880s. Thus it is hardly surprising that some Symbolist qualities should have crept into Renoir's work, and this produced the disquieting undercurrent which runs through his painting of the 'harsh' period. Significantly, the Symbolist poet Mallarmé was a close friend of the Impressionists, having as early as 1876 written a know-ledgeable article on Edouard Manet and the group, and during the 1880s Renoir dined regularly with him at the gatherings held by Berthe Morisot and Eugène Manet. In 1887 Mallarmé planned an edition of his poems which was to have been illustrated by his painter friends, including Renoir, Morisot, Degas and Monet, but it was never realized. The *Young Woman with a Swan* has an apt alternative title, *Apparition*.

(above left)
74 *Nude Woman*
LONDON, British Museum (De Hauke bequest). c. 1885–90. Red chalk heightened with white on Ingres paper. 38·5 × 30·2 cm. Signed lower left: Renoir.

The distinctive texture of Ingres paper can be clearly identified in the dark area where the nude is sitting; the chalk has caught on the tops of the tufts of paper, leaving unmarked the furrows and thus revealing its regular horizontal indentations and widely spaced verticals. The tiny zig-zag scribbles near the right edge level with the head are where the artist was testing the cleanness of the edge of his red chalk.

(above right)
75 *The Coiffure*
PALM BEACH, collection of Joan and Lester Avnet. c. 1895–96. 56 × 45 cm. Signed lower right: Renoir.

This unfinished work is a useful basis for the study of Renoir's methods during the 1890s, indicating a thin washed lay-in over a creamy-white ground and rapid summary brush-in of the form. Then the artist concentrated almost exclusively on working up the head in detail, with only a rough halo of colour around it to establish a background from which the head moves forward. His next step would probably have been to have completed the flesh areas, painting the clothes and background in last.

77 *The Painter's Garden at Cagnes*
GLASGOW, Glasgow Art Gallery and Museum (bequest of William McInnes). c. 1905. 33 × 46 cm.
Signed lower right: Renoir.

Renoir's failing health made it essential for him to live in a warm climate, away from the damp
cold of Paris; between 1903 and 1908 Renoir lived on the Mediterranean coast at Cagnes, in the
Maison de la Poste. Here he found again the light he had so loved in Italy, and the luminosity of
the south was to permeate his work for the rest of his life.

(*opposite*)
76 *The Renoir Family*
MERION, Barnes Foundation. 1896. 175 × 138 cm. Signed lower left: Renoir.
Photograph copyright 1977 by the Barnes Foundation.

This painting shows Renoir's family in the garden of the 'Château des Brouillards', where Renoir
was then living, in Montmartre. His wife and first son Pierre are to the left, while at the front
Gabrielle, Renoir's model and nurse for his son Jean, supports the two-year-old child. To the right
is the daughter of the writer Paul Alexis, who lived next door to Renoir.

78 *Portrait of Ambroise Vollard*
LONDON, Courtauld Institute Galleries. 81 × 64 cm. Signed and dated upper left: Renoir 08.

Vollard was a famous collector and connoisseur who began dealing in the early 1890s and bought large numbers of Renoir's paintings. His biography of the artist, however, cannot be considered entirely accurate (see Rewald, 1973). In this portrait Vollard holds a statuette by Maillol.

(*opposite*)
VIII *La Roche-Guyon*
ABERDEEN, Art Gallery and Museum. c. 1885. 48 × 55·5 cm. Signed lower left: Renoir.

Renoir spent two months at La Roche-Guyon, on the Seine near Giverny, in the summer of 1885 and a further two weeks there in the following July 1886; it seems likely that the Aberdeen painting dates from the longer stay in 1885. That summer the Renoir family was joined by Cézanne, who came with his family to stay with them, and together Renoir and Cézanne worked on motifs in the surrounding countryside. The influence of Cézanne, who encouraged Renoir to adopt a more structured paint surface, can be seen in this landscape.

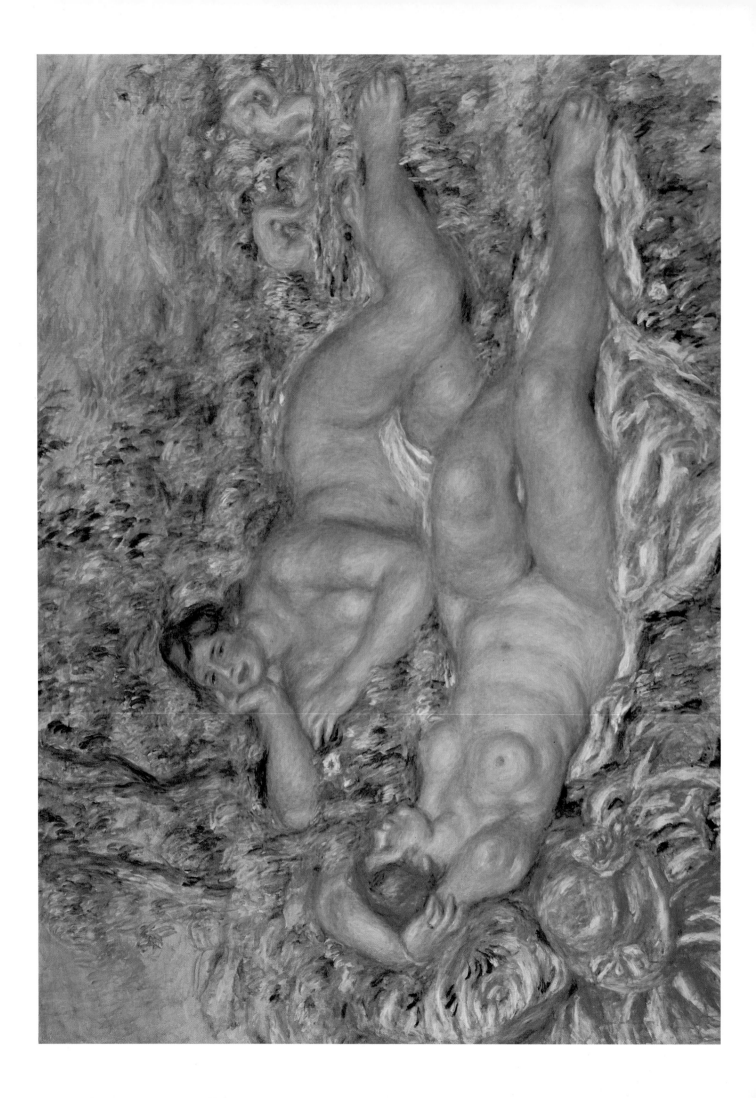

79　*The Judgement of Paris*
TOKYO, private collection. 81 × 99·9 cm. Signed and dated lower right: Renoir 1908.

Many of Renoir's works of the late period are based on classical themes, making no secret of his love of tradition; here Paris awards the golden apple to Aphrodite while Hera and Athena look on with affronted surprise. As in the usual classical interpretation of this theme, three nudes expose different views of their sensuously curved, full figures, thus exploiting the beauty of the female form to its fullest.

(*opposite*)
IX　*The Bathers* or *Nymphs*
PARIS, Musée du Louvre. 1918. 109·5 × 160 cm. Unsigned.

Among his last works, *The Bathers* was posed by Andrée Hessling ('Dédé'), who later married Renoir's second son, Jean. In order to work on canvases of the size of *The Bathers*, Renoir had a special easel made, 'where, on a kind of endless screen mounted on rollers, he could work on a large scale' (André), with the canvas being rolled round as he painted.

80 *Dancer with Castanets*
LONDON, National Gallery. 155 × 64·8 cm. Signed and dated lower left: Renoir 09.

The pair to this painting, the *Dancer with Tambourine*, is also in the National Gallery, London. The model for the latter and for much of the *Dancer with Castanets* was Georgette Pigeot, while the head of this painting was posed by Gabrielle (see Plate 76); according to Mme. Pigeot, the original conception for this pair had the models carrying dishes of fruit, as they were destined for the dining room of Maurice Gangnat. However, the idea was abandoned on the basis that the family might move house, which they eventually did. Renoir considered Gangnat among the most discerning of his collectors, and these paintings are two of the finest of Renoir's late works.

(*opposite*)
81 *Mme. Renoir with her Dog Bob*
HARTFORD, Wadsworth Atheneum (Ella Gallup Sumner and Mary Catlin Sumner collection). c. 1910. 81 × 65 cm. Signed lower left: Renoir.

This sensitive portrait shows Renoir's wife only five years before her death; she never recovered from the shock and anxiety of having her two sons Pierre and Jean away at war and both seriously wounded. Her rounded figure of the 1880s (see Plate 53) developed a warm motherly fullness, and her tanned complexion shows all the vigour of her peasant stock. Originally a milliner, Aline Charigot came from a background not dissimilar to Renoir's, but from the countryside of the Aube, at Essoyes, rather than from a large provincial town. The strong texture of the canvas grain is here clearly visible over the whole area of the picture surface.

82 *House among the Trees at Cagnes*
PARIS, Musée du Petit Palais. c. 1910. Watercolour on paper. 18 × 26·1 cm. Signed lower left: Renoir.

This was one of the views from Renoir's estate at Les Collettes, Cagnes. There is an oil painting of the same subject, dated 1910, in the Durand-Ruel collection, Paris.

(*opposite*)
83 *Bather Drying Herself*
TOLEDO (OHIO), Toledo Museum of Art (gift of Mrs. C. Lockhart McKelvy). 1912. 65·4 × 55·9 cm. Signed lower right: Renoir.

This is a superbly relaxed and sensuous figure study, an excellent example of Renoir's late technical virtuosity. He achieved a strong degree of integration between figure and landscape, in part through the degree of abstraction he used to portray the background, which, however, has more life than that in *The Large Bathers* (Plate 72), but mainly through the technical unity of the whole canvas. Dark transparent hues provide the shadows in the figure, while the roundness of the form is built up in thin, semi-opaque scumbles. Depth is suggested by the inclusion of the tree, upper left, which contrasts with the dark 'curtain' of foliage surrounding the figure, strengthening it and bringing it closer to the spectator. Renoir's fluid washes of transparent oil colours over a white ground are close to watercolour technique, and it is interesting to note that a white porcelain palette used by Renoir is preserved in the artist's studio at Les Collettes. While it is not known if Renoir used this palette for watercolour only, it seems likely that someone of his technical abilities would have become aware of the problems in judging oil colours mixed on a brown wooden palette which were to end up on a brilliant white surface. Although an artist of his visual powers and familiarity with colours would doubtless have been skilled in gauging the change in effect, it is interesting to speculate on whether he used his white palette also with oils. Surviving photographs would indicate to the contrary, as the artist appears always with a wooden, usually rectangular palette.

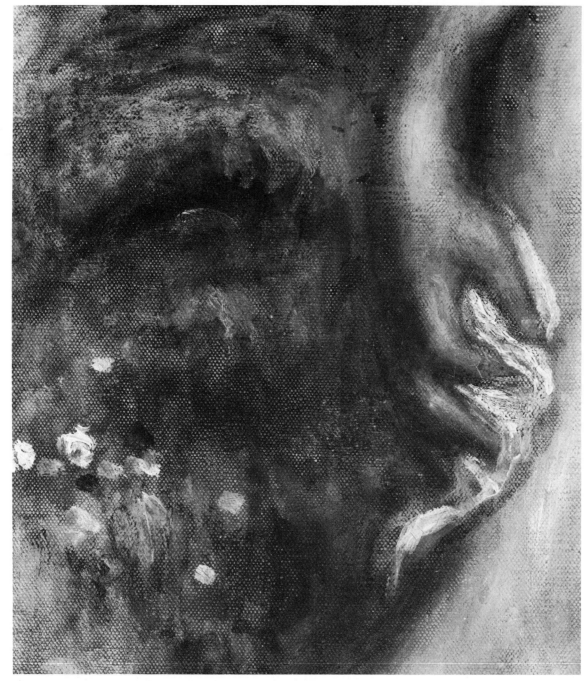

84 *Bather Drying Herself,* detail of Plate 83

Renoir's technique in creating the sense of form is clearly visible in this detail of the right hand, far left. The sharp clarity of the washed-in darks trapped in the canvas indentations should be compared with the misty, veil-like quality of the translucent flesh tones laid-in where the form 'turns' towards the spectator. More intense highlights emphasize the fingers, and the fabric of drape is caught in deft impasted strokes, where the loaded brush was dragged thickly across the textured canvas surface, allowing the deeper shadowed layers to vibrate through it.

(*opposite*)
85 *Bather Drying Herself,* detail of Plate 83

In this detail of the top of the bather's head and shoulder, against foliage, the canvas texture was again exploited, with dark washes over the white ground to add vibrance to surface, which emphasizes the technical unity of the work. The washes contrast with short dabbed strokes and the arabesque of white above the head. Small hairline cracks have appeared in the thicker impasto of the shoulder, possibly revealing an incompatibility with the darker layer visible beneath. The dryish dark touches representing the curls of hair lying across the model's cheek were evidently a late addition over dry paint.

86 *Vénus Victorieuse*
PARIS, Musée du Petit Palais. Bronze. Sculpted by
Richard Guino. 1915–16. 180·3 cm. high.

The artist's son Pierre told Pach the story of Renoir's
relationship with his Mexican sculpture assistant, who
made the works when Renoir's hands were too crippled
to use. The modelling was done under the master's
guidance, although neither spoke the other's language:
'A sketch on paper or canvas by Renoir would furnish
the general set-up of the mass of clay. With a light wand
the old man would indicate how work was to continue, at
one place making a mark on the *maquette* where the
modelling tool of the young sculptor was to cut away an
excessive volume, at another place showing by a pass
through the air how the contour was to swell out by the
addition of more material—which the nimble fingers of
the assistant moulded on until the desired form was
achieved . . . They communicated by grunts when the
thing got so close to the definitive result that it grew
exciting,' as Pierre Renoir described the scene. 'My
father would say, "Eh, eh eh—aaah! *ça y est*," and the
sculptor would be making his little jabs with the tool, so
much like my father's brush strokes that you'd think the
work came from his hand, as indeed it almost did . . .'
The watercolour drawing of 1914 (Paris, Musée du Petit
Palais), which was the first idea for this sculpture, was
inscribed by Renoir: 'The base of the statue should be at
the level of the water with small rocks and aquatic plants'
thus indicating the artist's original conception for the
setting of this figure. The theme of *Vénus Victorieuse*
follows on from Renoir's *Judgement of Paris* (Plate 79),
showing the victor in Paris's contest triumphing over her
rivals. It is significant to note how successfully Renoir's
solid painterly treatment of female form translates into
the medium of sculpture.

87 *After the Bath*
PARIS, Durand-Ruel collection. 1918. 38 × 41 cm. Signed lower right: Renoir.

This delicious painting combines both rich impasto with the thinnest veils of pure colour; the sky section was worked in these transparent washes over the white ground and strong canvas texture, while the figure and surrounding landscape were predominantly executed in a build-up of impasto over washes. The palette is one of the richest and purest of Renoir's late years, with separate touches of brilliant hues placed next to each other. Although Renoir still sometimes used black, this painting is entirely free of it, with the few darks simply using touches of ultramarine. The overall tonality of the picture is astonishingly bright and luminous, and the unity between figure and landscape, through the rich and harmonious palette, is one of his most successful.